Is There
a Man
in the House?

Dr. Charles F. Stanley

This book is designed for your personal reading pleasure and profit. It is also designed for group study. A leader's guide with helps and hints for teachers and visual aids (Victor Multi-use Transparency Masters) is available from your local bookstore or from the publisher at $2.25.

VICTOR BOOKS

a division of SP Publications, Inc., Wheaton, Illinois
Offices also in Fullerton, California • Whitby, Ontario, Canada • London, England

Second printing, 1978

Scripture quotations are from the *King James Version*.

Library of Congress Catalog No: 77-80948
ISBN: 0-88207-753-8

VICTOR BOOKS
a division of SP Publications, Inc.
P.O. Box 1825 • Wheaton, Ill. 60187

Contents

Preface

America has experienced one crisis after another since its founding over 200 years ago, but none is more threatening to the welfare of our nation than the disintegration of home life in our time. The principal components of a nation are its family units. As the family goes—so goes the nation.

I believe that our society's widespread civil disobedience, disregard for parental authority, immorality, and other lawlessness are the direct result of modern man ignoring a basic spiritual principle—God's design for marriage and the home. And the blame for our present dilemma rests squarely on the shoulders of our nation's men because they have been designated by God as the heads of their families. Is that too harsh a judgment? Not if you read your Bible as I read mine—and if you see the great opportunity that accompanies our responsibility. This book is for men—Christian men, specifically—since only they can build solid foundations in homes that support a righteous nation. When we men enact our true role, the foundational principles of our society will not be strenuously violated by frustrated groups such as the Women's Liberation Movement, whose members struggle for "equality" with men only to find themselves losing their cherished place of honor.

Socially and spiritually, the hour is late for healthy homes in America. My urgent plea is: "Will the real man stand up? And stand, please, before it is too late."

1

The Real Man

In the privacy of my pastoral office I heard the plaint that launched me on this venture to reclaim man's place under God's sun. A female member of my congregation sat before me, single, frustrated, lonely, and teary-eyed. Having just reached her 30th birthday, she saw in her future nothing more than protracted emptiness. It was not long before I realized that her idea of a happy future centered in marriage.

After listening to her reasons for feeling that she should marry soon, I asked, "Exactly what type of man are you looking for?" Without hesitation she exclaimed, "A total man." I commended her for her choice of words, while wondering if she was thinking about the male counterpart of one of those "total women." Then I asked, "Just what is a total man? How would you describe the man you are seeking for a life mate?" Thirty minutes later she had completed her description—of a breed of man that does not exist except in some maidens' imaginations.

The Ideal Man

Since that time I have asked many women the question I asked the young woman in my office, only to find their descriptions unsatisfactory. Women usually visualize the ideal man as a strong, healthy, well-dressed, good-looking, aggressive, successful, dependable, and responsible businessman. He is interested in all things and excels in most. He loves only one woman, but charms them all. And most excellent of all, he is a superspiritual leader in his home. Have you ever seen anyone who answers this description? Take heart, friend. Neither has any woman. Besides, it presents a distorted picture of the truly complete man.

What is a "total man"? He is one who understands and accepts the responsibility for the development of his mental, emotional, and spiritual capacity and demonstrates this by his maturing attitude and actions in his personal life, his home life, his vocational life, his social life, and his spiritual life. Now read the definition again with yourself in mind and weigh the emphasis on the words *understands, accepts responsibility, development,* and *demonstrates.*

Being a complete man does not depend on background, talent, education, skills, or achievement. It has little to do with looks, size, shape, or age. If these qualities were the criteria, most of us would be eliminated. Neither is a total man measured by his time of arrival. Rather, he is a man on a journey, in a process, forging an experience. It involves a journey God has planned for every man. To find out what God our Maker intended for us, we must go to His revelation, the Word of God. A glimpse there at God's first perfect man will provide a focus for our understanding today.

Adam's Creation

According to Genesis 1:26, God created Adam for Himself—for His own glory, not man's. The Scripture says, "And God said, 'Let Us make man in Our image, after Our likeness.'" God could not have complimented man more than to make man like Himself. Man is the crown of God's creation. We need to recognize, therefore, that we were made for God and in His likeness and image.

We fulfill our eternal purpose when our lives honor God and reflect His glory. What pleases a human father more than to hear, "That boy looks just like you; he even acts like you"? God takes pleasure in spiritual sons who reflect His character.

God's Commandments to Adam

After God created Adam, He gave him three commands. First, Adam was to rule over the fish of the sea, the fowl of the air, and over all the earth (Gen. 1:26). Adam's domain was the Garden of Eden, a perfect place for a perfect man and his perfect wife.

Second, Adam was to reproduce. God said to be fruitful and multiply and replenish the earth and subdue it (1:28). Man was to bring forth children who likewise would glorify God.

The third command God gave to Adam was: "Therefore shall a man leave his father and his mother and shall cleave unto his wife, and they shall be one flesh" (2:24). That is, a man's wife is to be first in his earthly relationships. God has not repealed these commands. Today it is still a man's responsibility to rule his world, to produce children in the image of God, and to be faithful to his wife.

Psychologists generally agree that all of us are products of our homes. Many people think some traumatic experience in the past dominates our present condition, but the general atmosphere of our homes has set the direction and pattern of our lives.

As I counsel people in my church study, one of the questions I invariably ask is, "How would you describe your home life when you were growing up?" Seldom, if ever, does the answer center in a single incident, but is rather an outpouring of the feelings they recall about the atmosphere of their homes. Often such words as *critical, negative, loud, insensitive, unloving,* or *indifferent* are mentioned. Every home has its atmosphere, made up of the combined moods and modes of expression of its members. While each family member contributes to the atmosphere, it is certain that the husband and father has the greatest influence—even when it's by default.

Adam's Composition

The Bible says, "And the Lord God formed man of the dust of the ground, and breathed into his nostrils the breath of life; and man became a living soul" (Gen. 2:7). God's first man was made of dust—dust that is easily blown away. This fact should say something to overblown male egos!

God also breathed into man the breath of life, and dust took on eternal dimensions. Out of that handful of dust, God created a living soul, not just mortal flesh and blood, but a life that is linked to invisible reality.

The first two chapters of Genesis describe man as God made him to be; he is obviously different from the typical female's image of man. God placed in a dust-core body a soul with the capacity to think, to rule his domain, to love his wife, and to rear his children. Man's soul has emotions by which he feels the needs and desires of his companions. He has a will with which to make proper choices in the leadership of his family. Man has an awareness, an ability to discern the needs of family members as well as his own. His conscience is a guide to keep him properly tuned in to his Creator.

God's first man was neither holy nor unholy— he was innocent. His was an untried holiness, and only God's first man has ever lived in that condition. All people since then have been born

with a sin-prone nature. We have to live with this
carnal nature daily, but God has provided victory
over it. The innocence man lost in the Garden of
Eden—which made him less than whole—is
offered to us in God's perfect Son, Jesus Christ.

A man may have a perfect body, but if his emotions, mind, and will are not under the control of
God's Holy Spirit he will fail regularly and tragically as the husband and father God intends him
to be. God designed us not only to cope success-
fully with the material environment but to relate
harmoniously to other living beings. Man is endowed with a spirit with which he can communicate with his Creator. Any man whose body, soul,
and spirit are not dedicated to God is fatally
handicapped, and therefore he is not and cannot
begin to be an adequate husband or father. No
amount of money will atone for the absence of
the Spirit of God in his life.

Adam's Claim

Adam had the right—and obligation—to claim
total dependence upon God. The Lord said, "Be-
hold, I have given you every herb bearing seed,
which is upon the face of all the earth, and every
tree, in the which is the fruit of a tree yielding
seed; to you it shall be for meat. And to every
beast of the earth, and to every fowl of the air, and
to every thing that creepeth upon the earth,
wherein there is life, I have given every green
herb for meat: and it was so" (Gen. 1:29-30).

This is God's promise of provision for man.
God declared Himself the source of everything

the first man would ever need. His habitation was a gift—the utopian Garden of Eden. Good was plentiful and varied. Beauty enveloped him. Man was to be totally dependent upon God.

So it may be with the new man—even in swampy surroundings. God intends for us to live in dependence upon Him, looking to Him for every need. And we can instill in our children the truth of Philippians 4:19: "My God shall supply all your need according to His riches in glory by Christ Jesus." What He did for His first man, He will do through Christ despite our polluted environment.

Not only did Adam have the right to claim provision, he had the right to claim guidance for his life. The Scripture says, "The Lord God took the man, and put him into the Garden of Eden to dress it and to keep it. And the Lord God commanded the man, saying, 'Of every tree of the garden thou mayest freely eat: But of the tree of the knowledge of good and evil, thou shalt not eat of it: for in the day that thou eatest thereof thou shalt surely die' " (Gen. 2:15-17).

What kind of home would you have if you looked to God as the source of every provision? If you looked to God for divine direction of your family? If we husbands and fathers could see ourselves as channels through whom God wants to bless our homes with divine resources and direction, we would have homes of harmony, peace, and happiness such as the world has never known. If we could grasp what God intended for Adam in the beginning and know that

His desire for us is the same, each of us would be well on his way toward becoming a complete man.

Adam's God-given Companion

You may think God would not create anything that was incomplete, but He did. After He created Adam, He looked at His flawless man and saw a deficiency, though not a defect. The lack was a woman.

"The Lord God said, 'It is not good that the man should be alone; I will make him an help meet for him' " (2:18). Adam needed someone with whom he could share all that God had placed in and around him. He needed someone to love. Adam was made in the likeness of God with untried innocence, the totality of what man can be, yet there was no other human being with whom he could share his life. So from "the rib, which the Lord God had taken from man, made He a woman, and brought her unto the man" (2:22). Only then did God declare His whole creation "good."

The Scripture says a wife is a gift of God (Prov. 18:22). If you are single and looking for a wife, be careful that you get God's gift for you. Some men feel they got someone else's gift. Others do not feel they got a gift at all. God did not intend marriage to be that way, for He wants each marriage partner to be a gift to the other. A husband, whoever his partner is, may look at her as God's gift to complete him, not to "finish him off "

When harmony is missing, home life is a battle of wits to see who is going to win. God gave Adam a woman to complete him, not to compete with him. A gift is something received with gratitude; therefore, it is taken care of.

The Scripture also says that God gave Adam a woman who was part of himself—she came from his side. The Apostle Paul said a man should love his wife as he loves his own body, and no man ever hated his body (Eph. 5:28-29). When you said your marriage vows, you promised to have and to hold your wife for better, for worse, until death parts you (if you spoke the traditional pledges). And those promises were made not only before friends but in the presence of God, and are registered in the heavenly records.

God gave you a mind, a will, and a conscience to guide you in making the right decisions. Therefore, you are responsible for your decisions, whether right or wrong. If your life is incomplete, it is not because God made it that way. Though you may have made a mistake in choosing a marriage partner, your wife is still part of you. The physical consummation made the two of you one. When separation divides you, both partners suffer; each is torn apart.

God intends for a man to have the same relationship with his marriage partner that Adam had with Eve. The first man was a part of his wife, and she a part of him. Our problem is that we do not understand clearly the biblical image of a man. I am part of the woman I married. My wife is part of the man she married. If you are not willing to live as a part of the woman you married, your attitude needs to be changed because you *are* part of your wife and responsible to God for her.

"Incompatibility" between partners is an excuse unacceptable to God. Personality difference is no reason for tearing asunder what God has joined. Yet many couples seek divorce on the grounds of this polite expression.

What does incompatibility mean? Many say simply: "We don't like each other." The Scripture says, "Therefore shall a man leave his father and his mother, and shall cleave unto his wife: and they shall be one flesh" (Gen. 2:24). That means divorce and separation were not the will of God for Adam and his descendants.

Divorce is a sensitive issue today. Probably many brokenhearted people who have experienced the torment of divorce would not take the same path if they had it to do over again. God's pattern for His man and His woman is togetherness forever.

In marriage there will be tests and trials threatening to separate and tear you apart. God's design for marriage is that it be so tightly knit that nothing can pull it apart. I cannot say that firmly enough to people who are still unmarried. Divorce is one of the most tragic experiences in life. So think long and hard in choosing a partner; be sure that you are getting God's gift for your life.

The one word that best describes a man's responsibility for his companion is a four-letter word: *care*. Ask any woman what she wants from her husband above everything else, and she will probably say, "I just want him to care for me."

Care says much that love does not say, because today the word love does not have the same meaning it once had. To a wife, care says, "Whatever your needs are, I am interested in them and am going to do my best to provide them." That is what God intended for His first man. When God said, "Cleave unto her," He meant for Adam to separate himself from everyone else, if necessary, but not to separate himself from Eve. A wife is an integral part of her husband.

One hears many differences of opinion concerning the responsibility of husband and wife. Some people say, "I believe marriage is a 50-50 deal." But the Bible says the *man* is responsible for what happens in his home (1 Cor. 11:3). The husband is the head, or leader, of the wife. How is he to lead? With tender, loving care (see Eph. 5:23-25, 28-29).

Adam's Restriction

God said to Adam, "But of the tree of the knowledge of good and evil, thou shalt not eat of it: for in the day that thou eatest thereof thou shalt surely die" (Gen. 2:17). God had provided everything that man needed, but one thing in the Garden he did not need—the tree of the knowledge of good and evil. Amidst all the beauty and perfection of Eden one thing was off limits. We are all familiar with what happened. Satan intruded, Eve ate the forbidden fruit, and man fell into sin (see Gen. 3).

What should this say to fathers? It clearly

teaches that some things are off limits. There are some activities and events in which our families must not participate. Proper restrictions confine us to those things which bring joy, fruitfulness, and growth.

God wants to protect us from the awful pain that results from the knowledge and experiences of evil. Some fathers may say, "Well, we have to learn somehow." The Bible teaches that as fathers we are responsible for helping our families avoid the experiences that will lead them astray or to fall into sin, causing them pain and loss. Even though there will be suffering in every family, fathers still have the responsibility of setting moral boundaries for their families.

Adam's Conflict
Adam and Eve were happily married, the only couple who ever knew "heaven on earth." They lived in a state of innocence and bliss with no such thing as sin. They could do anything they pleased, which by their nature also pleased God.

Adam and Eve's family conflict began when a third party, Satan, deceitfully entered the scene. According to Eve's conversation with Satan, Adam had apparently instructed her not to eat of the fruit of the tree in the midst of the Garden, because she understood God's command not to do so. Genesis 3 exposes Satan's strategy: he persistently asked Eve questions that implied God was not telling her the whole truth.

There will be family conflicts whenever we begin to doubt the truthfulness of what God has

said or question His restrictions and command-
ments. When one partner or one child is out of
harmony with God's will for that family, a family
conflict is inevitable. God's command to Adam
was that he rule his domain; disaster struck when
Eve ignored her husband's instructions.

The conversation between Adam and Eve following Satan's victory shows the influential sway
of women over men. Satan had to *persuade* Eve
to disobey God, but Eve made only one simple
suggestion, "Have a bite," to cause Adam's
downfall. Because of their ability to influence
their husbands, wives have a grave responsibility. The woman who uses her influence wrongly
will manipulate her husband to her own regret.
Women can connive to get their way if they are
clever enough, evil enough, or un-Christlike
enough, but seldom are they happy with the results of their manipulation.

Many wives know exactly how to get what they
want. They know how to dress, what to say, what
to give, how to act, and where to go to obtain their
hearts' desires. Women who misuse the power
God has given them will feel Eve's pain. She
gained a knowledge of evil, and lost the gift of
innocence. Eve accepted direction from the
wrong source. Her authority was her husband,
but she took directions from an enemy, Satan. As
a result she received the devil's due—disillu-
sionment and death.

Three Results of the Fall
In every family conflict there is a loser. Here both

Adam and Eve lost their heavenlike home. "Therefore the Lord God sent him forth from the Garden of Eden to till the ground from whence he was taken. So He drove out the man" (Gen. 3:23-24). The man, created in the image of God and endowed with all the faculties to make his life complete, was exiled from paradise and sentenced to "hard labor" in the bramblepatch world.

Adam and Eve also lost the harmony in their family. When harmony, mutual support, and common goals are gone, is anything of real worth left? Nothing in the world is so sweet as a home with constant harmony among its members, and nothing as wretched as a home without harmony, joy, and love.

The third thing lost was Adam's honor as head of his home. He failed God as its responsible and faithful leader, and a dire consequence was hatred and conflict that cost one son his life and another a lifetime of guilt and fear.

Cain and Abel did not grow up in Eden, but outside the garden where their father earned a livelihood by the sweat of his brow, plagued by the sin-nature he received when he disobeyed God. Unless you and I strive to obey God in our homes, we will create a spiritually poisonous atmosphere that will infect our children with disrespect for authority, both ours and God's. Our disobedience today may become our children's rebellion tomorrow.

Adam had no problems before his wife fell into the devil's trap. He communed regularly with

God and enjoyed life in the garden with Eve and the animals. Doom invaded his home when Adam failed to shield his wife from their enemy, bringing disaster.

If you trace a problem in your home to its root cause, you will find the trouble issuing from the violation of a spiritual principle. Spiritual weakness makes our homes vulnerable, and the head of the home needs the full spiritual armor offered by God.

Adam had every advantage for being a success as God's first man, but he failed to protect his family against evil. If a man is not successful in his family, he will not be truly successful in any area. But if he is successful in his home life he is manifesting the qualities of the total man that God intended him to be.

You recall that my version of a total man is one who understands and readily accepts the responsibility for the development of his mental, emotional, and spiritual capacities, and demonstrates this by his maturing attitude and actions in his personal life, home life, vocational life, social life, and spiritual life.

As a husband, how is your progress toward real manhood? Wherever you stand, are you ready to move forward? I'm with you!

2

Man of Steel
—and Velvet

More and more, it is no longer true that "like
father, like son," because society is pushing them
farther and farther apart in interests and convictions. During the Vietnam War, as an example,
the college-age sons of the national Secretary of
Defense, Army Chief of Staff, Secretary of the
Army, and Secretary of the Navy all opposed
their fathers' war efforts. How embarrassing, and
potentially tragic!

Who is to blame for family breakdown? There
are many causes, but I believe we men must accept the blame. Some men who claim to be the
head of their homes simply have done a poor job,
and other men have altogether disdained the responsibility that God commissioned. The inevitable result is family disintegration. The founda-

tions of our society are crumbling today because our homes are deteriorating.

A British psychiatrist said he thought at one time the problem with American homes was that domineering women were trying to take over their husbands' role. Later he came to the conclusion that it was not simply a matter of women grasping for power, but their desire to take over before men ruined civilization. We may not agree with his opinion, but we must concede that something is tragically amiss in the American home.

The Responsible Man

We find in both the Old and the New Testaments that God gave man authority to rule his domain. Apparently many men are not aware that they remain responsible for their families whether or not they exercise authority in their homes. Aggressive wives have seized authority in many homes, relegating their easy-going husbands to bystander status. Quick-witted children take the cue and push Dad further and further into the background. To everyone's surprise, this doing-what-comes-naturally arrangement generates all kinds of problems.

Children are disobedient and disrespectful. Wives are anxious and frustrated, burdened with endless cares. Finances are often tangled or chaotic. Daily schedules are hectic and family communication is a bad joke. And when the ruling wife avoids these problems through sheer managerial skill, she fosters other maladies for the future.

What will the domineering wife say when her husband no longer shows any interest in major family decisions that have been removed from his hands? Or little interest even in the wife who has demonstrated her self-sufficiency so thoroughly?

And what will she do when her children show confusion over their roles as male and female, husband and wife, father and mother? One tragic result of female domination of the home is sexual deviance. Sons and daughters grow up in reverse-role homes subconsciously unwilling to identify themselves with their natural sexual model. Today homosexuals are so numerous and society so uncertain about moral standards that even homosexual clergymen demand their sexual preference be regarded as normal and as an optional life-style. Hasn't America heard of Sodom?

Samuel Liebowitz, longtime criminal court judge in New York, repeatedly counseled parents: "If mothers would understand that much of their importance lies in building up the father-image for the child, they would achieve the deep satisfaction of children who turn out well." The veteran judge urged a simple principle for reducing juvenile delinquency: "Put father back at the head of the family."

Sociologist Gibson Winter observes: "Our tendency today is to assume that we can eliminate the authority of husband over wife and yet retain the authority of husband-wife over the children. The Bible is more realistic about marriage than modern man, for the truth is that in disobeying the one hierarchy we destroy the other."

When a business fails, the head of the company is held responsible, not the man on the assembly line. As head of the home, we husbands and fathers are responsible for its condition, whether good, bad, or indifferent. Husband, you were made to rule your home—how is the project doing? All around us are broken homes, disillusioned divorcees, and lonely children. In many cases, the cause is men who refused to rule their homes.

You may head a well-ordered home but if not, you can still become the head of your home and the husband God intended you to be.

Writer Carl Sandburg described Abraham Lincoln as a "man of steel and velvet." There is no better description of the kind of man God wants you to be. Throughout the Old Testament we see that the men whom God used mightily were men of steel and velvet.

The Man of Steel

A man of steel is a *committed* man. As a husband and father, he is committed to three things: to provide for his family; to protect his family from anything destructive to their minds, bodies, and spirits; and to point his family in the direction of the will of God.

When William Booth, the fearless pioneer of the Salvation Army, was asked the secret of his success, he replied: "From the day I got the poor of London on my heart, and a vision of what Jesus

Christ could do with the poor of London, I made up my mind that God would have all of William Booth there was."

Nor was Booth's family neglected. His children followed his footsteps so closely that biographer Edith Deen declared: "No family in recent Christian history has served so diligently the poor and the outcast, the prisoner and the hoodlum, bringing to them the healing ministry of Christ."

Second, the man of steel is a man of *conviction*. He stands firm in what he believes is right. He studies the Bible and knows not only what he believes but why he believes. One of the serious problems in families is that fathers do not know their faith well enough to teach it to their children. Many will admit that they have done very little Bible study—excusing themselves with: "I never have been much of a student."

What employee, when asked to read a book of instructions, would tell his employer, "Sorry, but I never have been much of a reader"? A man of steel finds out his responsibilities and acts upon them. A father cannot expect his children to grow up with strong spiritual convictions if they have learned none from him.

A third quality of the man of steel is *courage*. Many sons and daughters do not observe decisive, forceful fathers in their homes. Children who ask their father's advice should receive an answer though it may be unwelcome. Andrew Carnegie said, "To be popular is easy; to be right, when right is unpopular, is noble." There are times when father needs to say to his family, "That is *not* what we are going to do." The man who fears upsetting the apple cart has already upset his family through indecision.

What could be more inspiring to a child than a courageous father? A boy may say to his friends, "My dad's not afraid of anything," then see him back away from a family decision. Wrong decisions are better than no decisions by the family leader.

Fourth, the man of steel is a man of *character*. He is a man of integrity, one who can be trusted. He will do what he says. He is a man of moral purity who keeps himself for one woman. He is a man of honesty. A man of sterling character is one whose son will say, "I hope I can be that kind of father." His daughter will say, "I hope I marry that kind of man." Steel implies the trustworthiness and responsibleness of the man of sterling character.

A man of character is also masculine, not effeminate. God made the distinction between men and women very clear: "Male and female created He them" (Gen. 1:27). He didn't want men and women to look, act, and dress alike, with the intention of minimizing the differences. If we are honest, we will admit we prefer feminine women. To be masculine means to speak like a man, to move like a man, to think like a man, to act like a man. That is the way God made man.

A man of steel is *constructive*. He tries to build up others, especially the members of his family. He spends time with his wife and children. He builds up his business. He builds up the believers in his church fellowship, whatever his place of service. The man of steel sees himself as a constructor of society, his home, and his church.

Dad, let me ask you: When you come home after a rough work day, do you slam the door and stalk through the house without a word? That is a destructive attitude. Many fathers are destroying their homes not so much with words but with attitudes conveyed by their actions. What they fail to do causes as much destruction as what they do. A hardheaded, hardnosed, self-willed father who is determined to do everything his way and who has no time for his children, is cold granite, not tempered steel.

A man who is building up his family knows their needs and is striving to meet them. By "train up a child in the way he should go and when he is old, he will not depart from it" (Prov. 22:6), the Bible directs us to carefully guide a child in the way *that child* should grow. All children are different, and they cannot be treated alike. We must train each child according to his God-given temperament and qualities. The man who is concerned about building up his family makes it his business to know how his child thinks and why he responds as he does at various ages. He seeks to understand his wife and to know why she acts the way she acts. Knowing what makes a family tick takes a lifetime of learning and understanding.

Another important quality is *confidence*. This does not mean cockiness. The man of steel is, first of all, confident in God—confident that the heavenly Father is his God and his Sovereign, Provider, Protector, and Guide. He is confident of God's presence and leadership in his life. He is self-confident only because Christ dwells in him and he in Christ Jesus, through whom he can do anything that God wants him to do. He is confident in his family's love. A man of steel knows where he is going and that God will help him get there. He expects each member of his family to find God's will for their lives, according to Romans 8:28—"We know that all things work together for good to them that love God, to them that are the called according to His purpose."

One final fact about the man of steel: his life is *controlled*—its pivotal point is obedience to God. Under God's control, he brings his mind in tune with God's thoughts. His emotions are under control, to feel what God would have him feel. His body is under control, yielded as a living sacrifice to God. Unless we are suffering from a debilitating disease, you and I owe our families a healthy father and husband, mentally, emotionally, and physically. A man of steel takes steps and avoids certain actions to keep himself in top condition. He realizes that his family needs to depend upon him; he is not willing to cause his family suffering by self-indulgence.

You may think, "I am batting near the top because I believe in all those qualities of steel." Congratulations, but the game is only half over—you still face the left-handed slants of the man of velvet. That's the other half of the whole man.

The Man of Velvet

In spite of the strong qualities of steel, a man who lacks velvet traits is hardly fit to live with. Steel is not comfortable nor caressable; for human relationships we need responsiveness and sensitivity, the man who *cares*.

Care is not shown just by providing an income for the family, a spacious house for them to live in, stylish clothes for them to wear, and sporty automobiles for them to ride in. None of these things necessarily say, "I care." Saying "I care" means giving ourselves to them, because giving yourself says "I have time for you." Honestly, now, how many times recently have you taken your wife into your arms while your mind was racing on other tracks? We've all done it— perhaps without realizing that it betrays how much we care.

Our families need to know that we care. I have seen poor families with happy, sweet spirits, because the children think their father is number one, even though his income may be the lowest on the street. It is not the things that he gives his family but the care he expresses that says, "I love you." Care is a friendly touch, a whisper of something sweet, a word of encouragement, a solicitous telephone call. Genuine care, for which there is no substitute, may be expressed in myriad ways.

The second quality of a man of velvet is *consideration.* He takes time to find out the needs of others.

In a church where I was a guest minister, a

young college student came to me and asked if she could talk with me for a few moments. "I have grown up in a home where my father provided everything we needed," she began. "He is a Christian, the head of our household, but he doesn't know how to be considerate of his children. He has all the answers before we even ask the questions, and when I ask him for advice I get volcanic spiels on what I ought or ought not to do. All I want my father to do is let me tell him how I feel, but he won't let me."

It happened that I was planning to see this girl's father in the near future, so I asked permission to share her feelings with him. She said it would be all right, but she was not sure she could stand the consequences.

When I had the opportunity to ask this man about his daughter, he said that she was doing fine—"couldn't be better." "Would you like to bet?" I asked. He wanted to know what I meant.

"We've been friends a long time, so I'll lay it on the line," I said. "Your daughter doesn't feel the way you described at all." And I repeated what she had said to me.

His first reaction was defensive, to which I answered, "Wait a minute. You may think you are right, but if your daughter feels that you never hear her or consider her, whether you do or not is not the issue. The problem is that she doesn't know that you care."

We may put check marks by all the good things we have done, but if our wives and children feel we are not considerate then we *are not* considerate. If you think your family demands too much, you must find ways to reduce those demands to a point acceptable to everybody. Yet the problem usually goes deeper. Family members may be demanding because some basic need has not been met. A child is not likely to be over-aggressive if he has had care, love, and consideration.

One of the surest ways to show your care and consideration is to take a few minutes each night to ask your son or daughter, "How are you doing? Tell me what's been happening today." Then *listen*. Let your children know that you consider their feelings. Develop sensitivity. You know that something is wrong when your wife is not saying anything. The same is true of your children. When your child comes in from school, knocking, shoving, and carrying on before going to his room —he may have flunked a test; nothing has gone right—what is your reaction? You may want to scold him, but scolding will not meet his need. More than likely his day at school was similar to your day at work. Does scolding help you feel better?

We must remember that our children have feelings. Ten-, 11-, 12-, and 13-year-old children get upset too when they feel they have been mistreated. To scold them at that time intensifies their anger. We should say, "Tell me what happened. Did someone mistreat you? What can I do to help you?" Nothing stabilizes a child so much as knowing that his father cares what happens to him. The man who is velvet in character takes time to listen. It is not how much time he gives but the quality that counts.

The third trait of a velvet man is that he is *cooperative*. There are times when every member of the family wants to do something you would rather not do, and cooperation at the top is called for. At our house we have "pow-wows." I am the chief and have the final authority; nevertheless, we take a vote and I give due consideration to what the other members think. If I am outvoted on a matter that involves a violation of principle, I override the vote. But, if it is a matter of choice involving pleasure, I yield to my family's wishes.

A man's quality of steel does not mean that he is to domineer; the velvet of cooperation balances the steel of authority. No woman wants to snuggle up to a rock, and no child wants to play with a stone. A rock is abrasive, but velvet soothes and relaxes. A woman may admire the strength of steel, but she loves the feel of velvet. A cooperative man is gentle and good-hearted. He bends over backward to get along. Remember that a rock cannot bend—it breaks. Many families have at their head heartless stone instead of a man of velvet and steel. Such a man knows that family life cannot be all grit and valor, and he knows when to yield and smile.

Every smart man allows himself to be manipulated for innocent purposes. If you are so hard that you refuse to bend, you are missing some of the finest joys of life. Every child likes to think he has gotten the best of his father once in a while.

Every sweetheart, mother, son, or daughter needs to have his or her earnest desire occasionally. The cooperative man makes concessions, never against principle, but simply to please. He understands the difference between cooperation and compromise.

The man of velvet is a *communicator*. Most men can communicate better with other men on their jobs than with their wives. Perhaps this problem arises from the fact that a man knows the nomenclature of his business, but is not practiced in the language of relationships, so he remains quiet.

Many women ask, "What can I do to get my husband to talk?" Though I am sometimes tempted to reply, "Be quiet for ten minutes," I know what they are saying. Sometimes a man doesn't have anything worth saying, and sometimes he's too weary to talk, but the man of velvet will make the extra effort to keep communication channels open.

My son taught me a real lesson in communication. As we rode down the expressway on the way to church one Wednesday night, suddenly my son stopped in the middle of a sentence and said, "Dad, you are not listening." I had to admit he was right. My mind was on something at the church, and my son noticed I was too busy for him.

Communication is not just talking; it is also concentrated listening. As a man of velvet, you are going to have to listen to much that you do not particularly want to hear. Velvet says, "I can be reached at all times; I care about what you think." A family needs a father and husband whose ears are open. He may not understand everything or take everything seriously, but at least he is listening, because he has a listening heart. If your children have told you, "You are not listening, Dad," and turned away, something serious is wrong with the velvet side of your life.

A man of velvet also has the *conduct* of a gentleman. I have noticed husbands say and do things that are very unbecoming to a gentleman. Perhaps their attitudes reflect the general lack of courtesy which mars our whole society. When a woman enters a room where no seats are available, many men will not offer their chairs. Today, many women mow the grass, wash the car, paint the house, and even fix the furnace. If there is no man around the house, and if a woman enjoys mowing the grass, that is understandable. But a gentleman looks upon his wife as someone very special and is careful what he allows her to do. The Bible teaches that God made the man stronger than the woman. In some countries, women work power tools on the streets and climb on scaffolding to paint far above the ground. Is that what you want your wife to do?

Our concept of womanhood and manhood and the differences between the two is becoming very distorted. If women want to do heavy work, men will probably let them, but I do not believe a man can justify making his wife do "men's chores." When women feel they are forced to perform heavy tasks, they may be producing with their hands but rebelling in their hearts. Your wife may be cutting your grass with a lawn mower and mangling your reputation in her mind. God made women to be feminine, and a man of steel and velvet is careful what he asks of his wife.

The man of velvet may even *cry*, revealing compassion and tenderness. Do you remember that Jesus, the perfect Man, wept? There are times and reasons for weeping when one truly understands this heartrending world. Gibraltar is cleansed, not weakened, by the showers that stream down its face.

Abe Lincoln, "the man of steel and velvet," once said, "There is just one way to bring up a child in the way he should go, and that is to travel that way yourself."

3

A Good Provider
—and More

The typical American husband may acknowledge that he is not the citizen he ought to be nor the romancer his wife would like him to be, but he will loudly proclaim he is "a good provider for my family." He means that he works hard to provide all the material needs of his family. More than likely he has not seriously asked himself the question: "What provision for my family would benefit them the most?"

One Halloween my house was egged by a teenager riding past in an expensive sports car. Having seen the boy in the act and lacking a taste for eggshell omelette, I phoned the police with a description of the car. In a few minutes an officer had the culprit in front of the house, and shortly afterward the father drove up. Immediately he began to scold his son for his prank and the embarrassment he caused his family. Then he made a statement I will never forget: "Son, I have given you everything you need and most of what you want, and now look at you."

One more father was exasperated and perplexed that generous expenditures on his son had not taught him decency and respect for others.

There are three areas of provision dependent on the father: material, emotional, and spiritual. Perhaps we should determine first the basis of this responsibility.

As Adam and Eve faced a new way of life outside the garden, God told Eve her husband "shall rule over thee" (Gen. 3:16). With Adam's ordained leadership came responsibility: Adam and his male descendants were to answer to God for their care of their wives and children. And it was not to be easy: "In the sweat of thy face shalt thou eat bread," He told Adam (3:19). That has been God's plan from the beginning.

The responsibility is just as clear for the followers of Jesus. "If any man provide not for . . . his own house," wrote the Apostle Paul, "he hath denied the faith and is worse than an infidel" (1 Tim. 5:8). Even haters of God usually accept this basic responsibility, declared the Apostle.

Providing for one's family is not all drudgery and pain, of course. God knows that man needs a challenge to enjoy life and to mature. Adam confronted a world of weeds, thorns, thistles, wild animals, and a varied climate that taxed his strength and ingenuity. The struggle forced Adam to mature as a man; daily demands ever since have nudged husbands and fathers toward responsible leadership.

Material Provision

One of the material needs we are responsible for providing is food. When guests in my home see the many vitamins and minerals on the sideboard, they may wonder if we are "health nuts." The problem today is not so much whether we provide enough, but whether we provide the right kinds of foods. With products emphasizing quick preparation and flawless taste, consumers are sacrificing nutritional values in food. We cannot take it for granted that delectable and even varied foods are adequate for health. Numerous books and helps to essential nutrition are available.

A second material need is clothing. Your family need not outdress your friends, but neat and decent clothing indicates respect for the body. Adequate shelter is also necessary, as well as a means of transportation in our mobile society.

Emotional Security

The total man recognizes and takes upon himself the total responsibility of provision. The material need is actually the least of the three essential needs of every family, though many husbands don't get beyond the first. In surveys concerning family matters, I have asked a number of women this question: "If you could pinpoint the most urgent need that you as a woman require to fulfill your emotional needs, what would you name?" Nearly every woman without hesitation has answered, "Security." You are responsible for providing a sense of security not only for your wife but for your children in their emotional life.

Security does not rest on a big salary and the impressive home and car it buys. Women tell me, "I don't need the best of everything; what I really want is my husband. I want him to share his life with me."

Security arises from the feeling that a responsible person cares about us. Security inspires this reaction: "He is interested in what I am interested in." Security deepens when the father says sincerely, "I need you to help me in this problem."

Nothing substitutes for security in a woman's life. Her security stems from her husband's devotion, trustworthiness, and consistency. The woman who cannot count on her husband's word and actions is hampered in giving herself to him as he would like. She may possess complete material security but suffer emtional insecurity. This can cause both physical and mental stress and breakdown.

Another emotional need is that of love and affection. How does a man show love for his family? The easiest way is by a look. Do you remember your courting days? You may have been sitting across a classroom from her, or at a table in a restaurant, and in one glance you transmitted a whole paragraph. If you have not learned to express your affection for your family through a loving glance, you would do well to learn.

Every Sunday during church services my two teenagers, seated in the second row facing the chair where I sit, invariably catch my eye just before I stand up to preach. Nothing gives me a greater feeling of reassurance than the twinkle in their eyes that says to me, "Dad, we are praying for you." That is love expressed with only a glance.

Love and affection can also be shown by a touch. The touch is an extension of the real you. If a look and a touch are vital, more so your verbal expressions. You ought to tell the members of your family that you love them, that you think you have the greatest wife and the greatest children in the world.

Husband, have you ever met a woman who does not like to be told that she is beautiful? There is not a woman or child who does not brighten up when paid a compliment. As fathers and husbands who are respected as heads of the home, we can give a word of commendation that will make the day for our wives and children. Love and affection live in the reaching out, touching, feeling, looking, saying, and giving of yourself to your family.

The third area of emotional need is understanding. This does not mean that a man must be able to understand women completely—no one is asking for the impossible! God made women mysterious, and we love them for it. Understanding means that we are willing to accept them just as they are and we are not forever trying to make them something else. When you are understood, you feel accepted.

Every individual is different. There may be something irritating about one of your children—especially as he or she is growing up—but understanding says, "I accept you though you perplex me." In the generation gap, the complaint, "My parents don't understand me" really means, "My parents will not accept me as I am. They reject me in my spiritual, moral, and philosophical struggles. They want to match me to their pattern." We must approve of our children even as we disapprove of their morally wrong actions, and lead them, not push them, to higher understanding and deeds.

A man provides for the emotional needs of his family by giving them his time. Time is a little word that says, "I am willing to get involved with you, Son." Time says, "Honey, I am willing to listen to you." Time says, "I love you so much I want to be with you when you need me." No father can bring home a paycheck large enough to buy his way out of giving time to his wife and children.

I have been guilty of putting my work first, and I rationalized by saying, "It's because I'm doing it for God." But if I am neglecting my family, God is not impressed with what I am doing for Him. Shared time says, "You are the most important thing in my life right now." Time together builds a oneness. Time with our families transfers our character and strength to them. If a father is never at home with his wife and children, how will they receive what he has for their maturing?

A father should not overlook the provision of pleasure for his family—vacations, camping or fishing trips, or whatever recreational activities delight their tastes and promote healthy emotional growth. To encourage and participate in family good times is not only the father's responsibility but his privilege.

Another emotional gift is attentiveness. This means concentration on what people say as they say it. A man in our church described "being attentive to his wife" this way: "Attentiveness is my standing still long enough to hear what my wife has on her heart, whether or not either one of us understands."

Many things claim our attention, so we have to work at being attentive. If you are so busy that you are unable to focus your attention on a family member who expresses a desire, joy, or need, I wonder if you are able to focus your attention on God! One of our problems in listening to God may be that we have not learned to listen to our family. What would happen if you said to your wife: "Speak, sweetheart, for your husband heareth"? God really wants you to listen to her, you know. She may even have a message from the Lord for you. So, listen!

Spiritual Need

The third main area of provision for which a husband and father is responsible is the spiritual need. This certainly does not mean running out to buy a Bible for everyone in the family. To provide for his family spiritually, a man must be a Christlike father and husband—not perfect but maturing. Our children do not need a lecture about Jesus Christ so much as a manifestation of Him in the head of the home.

A good provider will create an atmosphere in which his family is able to talk about spiritual things. A good place to instill spiritual principles is at the dinner table where everyone is relaxed and open to almost any subject. One of the greatest accomplishments of a father is to adroitly and pleasantly serve spiritual fare with the food for the body. As you apply spiritual principles to areas of their interests you build them up.

My most effective teaching is often done in the relaxed atmosphere of the dinner table, when one or the other of my children presents a personal problem or relates a school incident involving a friend. Time after time my son or daughter has said a few days later: "Dad, I appreciate the principle we discussed the other day. I discovered that it works." Practical application of a truth drives it deep into your children's seeking, maturing minds.

Provision in the spiritual area includes the father counseling his wife or children about spiritual things. You might say, "Since I don't read the Bible much and know little about spiritual things, I am going to send my wife and children to the preacher." A pastor does not mind helping your family, but if you are sending them to him as a cop-out, not willing to search out solutions, you are shirking a major responsibility as a father. If you are a father who desires earnestly to provide for your family, then you, not anyone else, are responsible for counseling those children in spiritual matters.

Finally, in the spiritual area, you are responsible for leading your family to a Bible-centered church where the teaching issues from the Word of God. Your church must not be one where you have to sift what is said and say to your family after you arrive home, "You can't believe this, but do believe that." You should be able to confidently discuss what the family has heard and elaborate on it to build up each other. If your church does not build your family spiritually, you are failing to meet your family's needs regardless of whatever else you are giving them. They need the fellowship of Christian families who love God and will love them.

Who is sufficient for all these things? Every man who puts Christ first! God made man with the capacity to provide totally for his family: physically by endowing him with muscles and a mind; emotionally to cope with the worries and the cares of family members through time and attention; and spiritually by dependence on the living Christ within the believing heart. "I can do all things through Christ which strengtheneth me" (Phil. 4:13).

Cautions
There are some cautions to be observed in providing for your family. First is excessive provi-

sion—providing more than is needed or good for them. Jesus said, "If ye then, being evil, know how to give good gifts unto your children, how much more shall your Father which is in heaven give good things to them that ask Him?" (Matt. 7:11) Under God, we can provide all that the family needs, and like God we should try to meet the family needs, and like God we should try to meet additional desires as wisdom dictates what is good. Provision may be excessive in the material, emotional, and spiritual realms when it smothers individual initiative, decisions, and growth.

The second thing to avoid is enslavement to provision: working day and night to provide for family desires far beyond needs. A father may do this because of the expectations of his wife. A social-climbing wife wants everything her peers have. A son may hint at rebellion if he doesn't get a car like his friend's. A father with a guilt complex may act unwisely when he constantly hears, "Everyone else has one," and take on a second or third job to supply things that will hurt his family emotionally and spiritually.

A third problem for the provider may be pride. The pressures placed on you because of neighbors having bigger and better things can wound your pride if you are vulnerable in this area. But the feeling that you need to compete materially to establish a reputation is an expression of misplaced pride. Jesus counseled: "A man's life consisteth not in the abundance of things which he possesseth" (Luke 12:15).

Many men's ulcers, heart problems, and other diseases are not the outcome of too many hours of work but of the emotional stress of clutching for the top. When a father's health breaks down, the family may become critical rather than being appreciative of what he has done for them. The reason is that they, like he, rate material benefits far above spiritual benefits, and when the flow of provisions is threatened they are more anxious about lost comfort than lost health. Poor dad—he can't figure it out because his values are distorted too.

A tragic sidelight to all of this is escape from provision. Every year more than 100,000 men walk away from their family responsibilities. Now, newsstories tell of many women doing the same thing. No normal woman whose needs are being met in her family life will walk out. Lazy men with no initiative, henpecked men with no dignity, and beaten men with crushed hopes fill this drifting stream of humanity. Somewhere they have been deprived of their manhood—and they never discovered a divine destiny. They are truly to be pitied, even as their sin of irresponsibility is to be condemned.

Imbalance in the vital matter of provision may have disastrous consequences. An overindulgent father may create in his child an expectation of getting anything just when he wants it. "Spoiled" is one way to describe this result.

If a father gives a child things too readily, that child will not feel the need to pray. And the child may learn to praise the Lord very tardily. He takes everything for granted, hindering his prayer life as well as his faith.

It is important to teach our children to wait upon the Lord. There may be some things our families want which are best to pray for and wait for. It is far better for a parent to deprive children of some things they want in order to teach the lessons of patience, prayer, and of trusting God.

An imbalance in provision disturbs the security of any family. Obsession with material things turns our attention away from God. You may ask, "What is too much? Only you know—or can know—what is best for your family. As fathers, we must observe our children, know our wives, and make a wise evaluation of the options. Together the family can set goals so that each one has some responsibility for the successful functioning of the home. God, through us, will provide all that is necessary.

If you are a father, I ask you: "If an adequate provider is a man who provides for the spiritual, emotional, and material needs of his family, would you say that you are a good provider?" If you are not a Christian, of course, you cannot possibly provide for your family fully because you cannot begin to meet their spiritual needs. If you are a Christian but are not walking in the Spirit, you are not able to provide fully for your family either. The total man is growing in his spiritual life, diligent in his vocation, and loving toward his family—thus reproducing whole persons in the family that God has given him.

4

God's Leader

The home is more than a house where people eat, sleep, and talk. The Christian home is a little society—an organization, a business, and a part of the spiritual body of Christ. It is far more complex than most people realize. The average man marries to enjoy himself, not realizing that he has taken on an awesome responsibility to lead his wife and his household. He has become the guide of a small organization, a social organism, which our Lord Jesus calls a family.

Today we see much confusion and frustration in our homes. One reason is that the man who should be the head of the home has never recognized his responsibility as leader. I hear married men say, "I'm just not a leader." Husband, if you are not a leader you are not fulfilling your destiny, because God requires leadership from a husband.

American families today are foundering in frustration, anxiety, and emptiness with vague goals and little sense of direction. This could well be the reason their rebellious children cannot wait to leave to make homes of their own. They are unhappy because they see no real purpose or meaning in their homes. The father is primarily responsible for this situation, not the mother or the children.

Today a major problem in the home is authority. Some challenge: "By whose authority has the husband been placed over the wife?" If you should ask "women libbers" what they think, they will say, "Some egotistical man contrived this and foisted it on society. It is unjust, and we are not going to abide by it." If you ask God, you will find that He designed the husband to be head of the wife and the family. Try as we might, we cannot improve upon God's design.

The Scripture teaches in Ephesians 5:22-23 that the husband is to be the head of the wife and the wife is to be in subjection to her husband. Many principles not spelled out are implied in this passage. First, the passage deals with God's announcement that the husband—whether he wants to be or not—is the leader of the home. The only question is whether he is *God's* leader.

The family is an organization which functions 24 hours of every day, 365 days of every year. It is one of the most unusual organizations in the world, and one of the most important. But strange things are happening to this organizational unit.

The average man comes home every workday evening, sits down to a palatable meal, watches television or putters with a hobby, and goes to bed to get up the next morning and repeat the same process with little conception of the human assets and liabilities he is handling in his family organization.

Corporation President

In your home, average husband, you are the president of a corporation with many divisions. Let me list some of them: accommodation, food service, transportation, education, worship, recreation, finance, counseling, medicine, and maintenance (which includes carpentry, plumbing, sanitation, painting, decoration, lawn service, and perhaps animal care). No other organization in the world attempts to operate so many divisions without a paid secretary! Nor does any other organization have higher standards for harmony, prosperity, and stability. Young men thinking of marrying should think more than twice. To become a husband and father is an awesome responsibility in the eyes of God.

God's objectives when He established the home were to arrange a companionship, a companionship of husband and wife and children that would build up each other. In so doing, all of them would be built up in Jesus Christ. If family members are growing, building, and learning in spiritual ways, they are continuously being conformed to the likeness of Christ.

One of God's objectives in growth is for each member to be motivated to rise to his maximum. A husband may rise to his maximum as family leader. A wife may reach her potential as her husband's helper, subjecting herself to her husband, "as to the Lord."

The wife who says, "I don't like the idea of being subject to my husband," has a streak of rebellion within her. As God places upon the husband the responsibility of headship of the home, He relieves the wife to become the total woman that He wants her to be. If she competes for the same position, authority, function, and responsibility as her husband, she is disqualifying herself for being the maximum woman she is created to be. God made man and woman equal in value and partners in subduing the earth, but different in their family roles; the wife will never be president in God's family structure.

If we reverse God's design, we hinder His purpose and His objective. The obligation of being the head of the home belongs to the husband even when he resigns the post. There's no leave of absence or early retirement in this organization. By virtue of birth and marriage, you have life tenure; you might as well get on with the job!

Some husbands object with the admission: "My wife is more talented and knowledgeable than I am. She has a better cultural background than I do." That may be an accurate observation, but family order is not based on intelligence or talent—it is based on God's decree given for the best interests of both husband and wife. We may not understand it, but we can accept it as the wise direction of a loving God.

Some new husband may be thinking, "I just got married; what kind of responsibility do I have?" The same. "But I don't have many responsibilities," you insist. Yes, you do!

The alarming thing about so many marriages today is the way people hop in and out of them. Obviously many do not know what they are hopping into, and the unexpected brambles send them running. Young people are getting the idea somewhere that marriage is only for pleasure. Marriage has a lot to do with pleasure, but no less with responsibility.

Some time ago I counseled a couple who were having marital problems. The man wanted to divorce his wife. When asked, "Upon what grounds?" he replied, "Well, I just feel that she'd be better off with someone who could provide better for her the things in life she wants. I'm willing to get out and let somebody else move in." I told him, "The problem with that route is that another man cannot fulfill your responsibility." Some wives make this mighty hard, but under God the husband is obligated and able to meet his wife's needs.

The Head

Part of our problems come from misunderstanding what the head of the home is. We're hearing a lot today about equality and inequality, inferiority and superiority in the family. God did not make man superior nor the woman inferior at the Creation. Not one single verse in the Bible suggests that. Conservative Christians are accused of holding women down and refusing to allow them to fulfill their potential. But Bible believers refer critics to Paul's word in Galatians 3:28. "There is neither Jew nor Greek, there is neither bond nor free, there is neither male nor female: for ye are all one in Christ Jesus." This establishes all Christians on the same level before God.

When God designates the husband as the head of the wife, He does not suggest the husband is superior or more intellectual or more capable in a practical way than she is. Some husbands may promote this interpretation, and some preachers may carelessly imply it, but God's Word does not support it. The question is not who is superior or more privileged, but who is the leader in God's family organization.

"Why do we need a leader?" some young people object. "Can't both husband and wife be leaders? Aren't we free to make our own choices?"

My answer is: try to name one project requiring careful decisions by a team of people that has been successful without a designated or recognized leader. All the way from playground competition to political campaigns, wrangling smothers action and individuality destroys unity unless one leader is recognized. Why do we expect the complex enterprise of marriage to be different?

The family has a God-ordained structure to

achieve its goals. This structure allocates authority, just as in a business venture. The president of a corporation is not necessarily superior to the vice-president in ability, but for the good of the vice-president and all other subordinates, cooperation is given to direction from the top.

First Corinthians 11:3 and Ephesians 5:22-24 give us a chain of command which starts with God. "The head of every man is Christ; and the head of the woman is the man; and the head of Christ is God." "Wives, submit yourselves to your own husbands, as unto the Lord. For the husband is the head of the wife, even as Christ is the head of the Church: and He is the Saviour of the body. Therefore as the Church is subject unto Christ, so let the wives be to their own husbands in everything."

Here we see the inconsistency of claiming independence and authority for wives. If we say the Bible is wrong in placing the man in authority over the woman, then we must say Christ is not the appointed leader of the Church, nor is God the Father necessarily the leader of the triune Godhead in its functioning. Yet, the rest of Scripture affirms that the Father heads the Divine Council, and that Jesus is the Lord of the Church. That reality establishes the remainder of God's chain of command as being: Father; Son; man; woman.

Despite their different roles in the divine hierarchy, the Father and the Son are equal. Jesus declared their equality with these words: "He that hath seen Me hath seen the Father," and "I and my father are one" (John 14:9; 10:30).

When Jesus walked this earth, He was obedient to His Father; we, in the same way, are to be obedient to Christ, and likewise the wife is to be obedient to her husband. From God's view, and He is omniscient, this hierarchy is the best arrangement for mother, father, and children. Of course, the plan does not work as God intended if the husband fails to love his wife as Christ loves the Church!

For the husband to be the head of the house does not mean he goes around beating his chest, expecting everybody to bow down and become his doormat. Subjection in God's terms means fulfillment of a master plan, self-expression within limits. Everyone who lives by God's plan is in subjection to someone else; each person needs to find his role in God's plan.

Plainly, God's role for the wife is to be in subjection to her husband. We can understand this better by investigating how the Church is to be in subjection to Christ. Jesus asked obedience from His disciples, but He welcomed their questions and honored their feelings. He set a standard of perfection before them, but He assured them of forgiveness and continued love in failure.

Peter was obnoxious, but our Lord tenderly disciplined and corrected him. At one time Jesus told Peter he spoke like the devil, but Jesus still treated him as a friend. Jesus always sought willing compliance instead of imposing His rightful authority on His followers.

I have never met a woman who wanted to leave

a husband who was a Christlike head of the home, one growing (not perfect), and exercising his responsibility in love. Women who want "freedom" or to "do as they please" have a basic problem of resistance to God. When we don't want to do what pleases God, we don't want to please others either unless it advances our self-interest. This attitude breeds frustration, anxiety, and an empty search for meaning in a wife who is confused about her proper role in the family. A true spirit of submission to God enables us to submit to others according to God's plan.

Deadbeat and Dictator

Our image of dad as the authority figure in the family has suffered two serious distortions. One is the man who wants to boss his family but doesn't want the many responsibilities that accompany the position. He is indifferent or insensitive to the needs of his family and is inclined to shy away from hard decisions. His remoteness and indecisiveness create insecurity in his wife and children. They never know what they can count on, and their idea of an authority is lots of talk and little action.

The other distortion is the father who rules as a dictator—an autocratic leader who permits no questioning of his decrees. His word is the first and the last. He rules supreme—but not in the hearts and thoughts of his browbeaten family. He boasts about running his family, but everyone knows he only maintains outward conformity. Behind his back, family members are ignoring him just as he ignores their feelings. When a man is the genuine head of his family, he doesn't have to prove anything to anyone; he is quietly obeying God and enjoying the results.

A dictatorial father may be a disciplinarian who knows no leniency, who rules by the word of his law, but he cannot claim such authority from God. Jesus Christ was patient, gentle, and loving. God says we are to rule our families as Christ rules the Church. Though His measures are firm, He acts always in love.

The man who wants to make all the decisions without discussion or counsel from others misses one of his greatest opportunities for guiding his children to maturity and his wife to contented partnership. Participating in decision-making gives younger members of the family a feeling of self-worth and confidence, essential qualities for becoming responsible and productive adults.

The autocratic father resists his family's opinions and ideas because he lacks deep-down confidence in himself. His poor self-image is threatened by any suggestion of criticism. Someone has shattered his sense of worth, and he blindly extends the destruction to his children. Some wives get the "nervous jerks" when they see their husbands coming because they don't know what to expect next. This male chauvinism is not supported by the Bible.

A father, whose son had been expelled from school for a whole quarter, asked me if I would have a talk with his boy. Sitting alone with the youth, I asked him to think about himself for a moment and then tell me briefly how he would describe himself. He broke a long silence with the dismal label: "A nobody."

The dejected boy continued to discuss his problem, but his first words had revealed his need. His father, an impulsive, quick-tempered, insensitive, dictatorial man, had destroyed the boy's sense of self-worth. Why should that boy want to please his father? Who can stand being treated as a nobody?

As fathers, we have to acknowledge that each of our children must be recognized as worthy, distinctive persons. They must be understood and accepted as they are. While a dictator makes no allowance for individual personality, the Christlike head of the home coordinates the varied abilities and weaknesses into a diverse unit helping each other and serving God.

God has specifically equipped the man for his role as leader to build up each member of the family. If you doubt this preparation, perhaps you need a refresher course under the Lordship of your Leader, Christ. Together, under Him, the family can become the maximum of everything God wants it to be.

When the wife has the opportunity of living in a happy, secure home under the leadership of a husband who looks to God, she relishes being an essential part of that family in the giving of herself. There the children grow up in the nurture and admonition of the Lord. As the wife accepts her place and responsibility, she is becoming the total woman that God wants her to be, a satisfied woman fulfilling her desires as a woman. She understands her personal equality with her husband and cherishes her advantages in God's plan. Fulfilling her role leads to her best opportunity for experiencing heaven on earth.

If you don't like the condition of your home today, you can improve it. But first there must be understanding of God's design for that home. Simply stated, His design is for the husband to rule his home in love, humility, and firmness—that is the man's part. The wife is to submit to her husband's direction without reservation and exercise all her abilities in coordinated partnership—but the husband must not try to force compliance, just as the wife cannot demand her husband's love. Role fulfillment must be voluntary to be real.

Of course, the leader will make mistakes—he and his wife must allow for this. But the man who is looking to Christ and is open to his wife's help will learn by his mistakes. That is the process of maturing. The wife need not worry about being responsible for her husband's mistakes. She is responsible for being submissive to her husband. God holds the husband responsible for his family kingdom. If he delegates authority and the delegated one "blows it," the husband is partly responsible. He is the one whom God will call to account for supervision of the home.

Management Policies
The husband, as chief priest of the home, has a personal ministry to meet the needs of his family.

There are ten practical things a godly leader in a home will do.

First, he will see himself as the family leader, as God declares.

Second, in consultation with his family, he will determine the policies by which the household operates: how much money can be spent, how late the children can stay out, standards of courtesy and modesty, etc.

Third, the godly leader will assume responsibility for his decisions or lack of them, not blaming others for his mistakes.

Fourth, he will delegate authority for carrying out policies, to his wife and the children according to their abilities and needs.

Fifth, the man will guide his family in setting individual and family goals, starting where they are now in experience and understanding. He will show each child the importance of keeping an eye to the future as well as acting prudently today. He will gather his family together to talk about ideas for their future, stressing the importance of each member playing his part to help the family reach these goals. A family will have financial goals, spiritual goals, material goals, social goals, and personal goals. This is a complex project which requires a substantial amount of time and a good deal of flexibility. My wife and I spent a week's vacation at it, and some of the effects will be seen the rest of our lives, I believe.

Sixth, a godly man will teach his children practical principles for everyday living that will accelerate their progress and spare them grief.

Seventh, he will be accessible to his family. Children often misbehave to gain attention. They need loving and attentive counsel. When the man of the house is too busy to attend to his household, they may despair that he doesn't care.

Eighth, he will forgive mistakes—till 70 times seven, though some judicious adjustments will be in order before the same mistake reaches that total.

Ninth, a responsible leader will lead his family in regular prayer and Bible reading to nurture spiritual life and relate all the family concerns to God. When a child wants to know, "How is life different because of your prayer and Bible study?" you will need a satisfactory answer based on your personal experience.

Tenth, the complete husband and father must learn to depend more and more upon the Holy Spirit for his daily guidance and power. Jesus and the Father sent the Spirit for this purpose. Submission to Him will make the difference between failures and successes, frustrations and fulfillments. Living by the Spirit will help you follow all the nine preceding guidelines even when you forget them.

Using Solomon's famous description of a praiseworthy wife in Proverbs 31 as a guide, a contemporary wife has written the following tribute to God's leader in the home:

Who can find a faithful husband, for his price is far above that of a Cadillac or even a Rolls Royce.

The heart of his wife doth safely trust in him

whether he is on a business trip, or comes home late from the office.

He tries to do the best for her and his family as long as he lives.

He learns to use the tools of his trade and isn't afraid of a hard day's work.

He is knowledgeable about world affairs and uses this for his family's enrichment.

He rises early in the morning for his devotions and asks for wisdom for his daily tasks.

He considers investments carefully and buys a home, property, or business with an eye toward the future.

He watches his health and gets the sort of exercise he needs in order to stay physically fit.

His work is of good quality even if he has to put in extra hours to make it that way.

He doesn't neglect his home.

He is concerned about social issues and tries to help those who are in need.

He isn't afraid of difficult times because he has learned to trust God and has done what he could to provide for his family.

He nourishes himself and his family both physically and spiritually.

His wife is well-thought-of in their community because he never belittles her.

He has a hobby that is relaxing and worthwhile.

He is strong and honorable and is a happy person, easy to live with.

His conversation is wise and uplifting. In

fact, he makes it a rule of his life to speak kindly.

He is interested in all things that concern his family and is not lazy nor indifferent.

His children love him and admire him, and his wife is proud of him and says,

"Many men have succeeded in this world, but you are the best of them all. If I had it to do over again I would still marry you."

Flattery is deceitful, and good looks are only on the surface, but a man who loves and fears God shall be truly praised.

This sort of man deserves to be treated like a king, for his life proves that what he believes is real.

— Gladys Seashore*

---

*Used by permission of the author and The Evangelical Beacon, © 1977.

5

Trainer in Residence

"Train up a child in the way he should go: and when he is old, he will not depart from it." Parents sometimes use this biblical proverb as an escape hatch from their recognized failures in raising their children. When prospects look ominous, parents clutch at this promise and remind God of the ways they led their children in right paths. In some families the nagging question remains unanswered for years: "Did we really train our child in the way he should go?"

As agonizing as this dilemma may be, such parents are still far better off than the ones who deliberately escape their responsibilities by actually abandoning the family or by becoming so preoccupied with side interests or careers that the children's training is neglected. The absence of the father or of his instruction leaves a void that may take years of experience and many mistakes to overcome.

From God's point of view, the only man who can count on seeing his grown-up children walking in God's way is the man who is attempting to follow the admonition in Proverbs 22:6—*training* his children in godly ways while they are young.

An obvious meaning of this proverb is that children will continue into adulthood the thought patterns and actions practiced when they were young. But the truth goes deeper than that: it is a promise that the power of good and of God known in childhood will exert control when the grown individual is free to make his own choices. The verse suggests God's faithfulness to His Word and mercy to His people.

Fathers are inclined to think, "My children are not so bad." Maybe they are not, but what is hidden in their minds and secret memories? Will their actions please you as they grow into more and more freedom? And will they please God? I cannot do anything after my children have left home, but I can impart that training while they are home and anticipate God's keeping of His promise in their adult years.

Some parents protest: "I can't believe that. My children were taught what was right in a Christian home, and look at them now. That verse cannot be true."

After I had preached a sermon on the home, a musician who had taken part in the service came to talk with me. He said he had provided well for his family and brought them up in the church, but that his 20-year-old daughter was causing heartbreak and misery for the entire family. He claimed to believe the Bible but added, "I don't believe that passage is necessarily true."

I responded that Proverbs 22:6 is true or none of the Bible is true and reliable. The problem is not with God's promise but with our training. Because children live in a home where parents are saved, where the essentials of life are provided, where members give money to the church, pray at meals, and read the Bible once in a while, does not mean Christian training is received.

Training Schedule

When I delve into a father's problems in his home, it often becomes evident that he is not training his children as he should. Even the atmosphere hinders growth rather than fosters it. Before renouncing the promise of Proverbs 22:6, let's see what is involved in training children. I want to challenge you with twelve positive possibilities in leading children in "the way they should go."

The first step is your own *faith* in God's promise—God is true to His Word, and Proverbs 22:6 is a part of His inspired Word. When I, to the best of my God-given ability, attempt to train my children properly, God is going to do His part.

Let's look at the reverse of the promise: if you train up a child in the way he should *not* go, what will happen? A father who is harsh, inconsistent, and selfish at home, though he carries his Bible to church and holds a church office, will produce resentful and rebellious children. By his unrighteous conduct he has trained unrighteous children. The only deliverance for these children is the grace of God reaching them through some other Christian's faithfulness.

Frequently I have heard pastors relate sad tales about their children and then add: " . . . in spite of all I have taught them." They perhaps didn't realize that telling and teaching are two different things, and a busy pastor can easily forget that training takes time and intensive effort. Failure to teach good things has consequences just as grievous as teaching bad things.

Second, a father must be a *Christlike example* to his children. Do you want your son to live according to your words or your actions? Both form your example. Many fathers say, "Son, here's what I would like you to do," and the son replies, "But Dad, you didn't do it that way." Someone has said, "A child does what his father tells him until he is 15 years of age and after that he does what his father does."

All of us have been training our children positively or negatively since we first held them in our arms. We trained them by what we did, how we did it, and what we said. You and your wife are the strongest influences in your child's life until you allow someone else to take over that role. How are you using it?

Someone asked a little boy if he was a Christian. He said, "No, I'm not. My daddy's not one, and I'm just like him." That's an immature child's honest response to a very serious question. Sadly, our negative influence is picked up more quickly than our positive. He is going to be like his father. Whatever we want our children to be, they must see it as well as hear it from us.

If you want your children to pray, teach them to pray by instruction and example. If you want them to read the Bible, you must read it regularly and live by it. If you want them to be kind, gentle, and considerate, you must be kind, gentle, and considerate. Children have their antennas out at all times.

A child's innate desire is to win the approval of his parents. He thinks, "If my father does it, he must like it; if I do it, he will approve what I do." Therefore he copies his parents in his early years. Everything he sees is a lesson in this early stage. This continues in diminishing degree to later years.

One Sunday evening as my son drove us to church I mentioned that the speedometer needle had passed the speed limit. "Well," he calmly answered, "we are running a little late and I've noticed that when you are in a hurry you usually drive about 65." I had taught him a bad lesson without realizing it.

Third, we fathers must *educate*. In Deuteronomy 6:7, God said to the nation of Israel: "You are to teach these precepts and principles to your children in the morning when they rise, during the day as they walk about, and in the

evening when you sit down to the table" (paraphrased). Can you name one principle you have
deliberately, determinedly taught your son or
daughter in the last 30 days? When did you con-
sciously attempt to teach a principle about life,
spiritual or pragmatic? There are some basic
truths and principles which we need to teach or-
ally and systematically. We are the God-given,
number-one teachers of our children.

Instruction needs to relate first to spiritual
things. Have you taken time to explain the way of
salvation to your children? Or have you left that
to Mom or the preacher or Sunday School
teacher? You are responsible for teaching your
children how to know the Lord, just as the pastor
is responsible for teaching you. You can never
shift that responsibility to anyone else.

Salvation is just the beginning, of course. The
Christian life is a growing venture, with spiritual
truths to be taught for every significant step in
growth. Are you willing to leave these crucial
lessons to others who may not get around to
them? I realize that your father may not have
taught you these truths, but now you know that
you are responsible for your own children.

And we need to educate in pragmatic matters
—how to handle money, for example. Though
you probably haven't mastered the subject yet,
you know a great deal more than your children
through experience, and you can save them
costly mistakes in this important area.

Teach your children about sex at an early age.
They need to know that it is for producing chil-

dren and also for pleasure—but it is a sacred and private experience between married people. Don't let misinformed friends provide distorted information in this vital phase of life.

Who will teach them about gentleness and kindness, courtesy and good manners? Perhaps their mother, but we need to explain why men treat women with respect and how God is pleased whenever we help a person in need. A son needs to hear from his father how to study— things like "study before play," tips on concentration, and the values of note-taking. We can't assume the schools are teaching this.

As I see the frightening things happening in our society, I shudder to think of children's values being formed by these outrageous examples. From rock music stars to political cheats, these people are influencing life-styles and making decisions that affect us all. Unless we retrain our children in some areas and protectively train them in others, they are going to break our hearts. We are their instructors.

Discipling my son has been one of my most exciting experiences. For a long time I had been caught up in the discipling of others; then the idea dawned: "Why not disciple the fellow who not only loves you but counts it a privilege to have you all to himself?" How richly rewarding this deepening relationship has been for both of us!

The fourth training need is in *love*. Love is active, unselfish consideration for the needs of others. Our children are starving for someone to love them. When a child grows up without a father's love, a sense of insecurity follows that child the rest of his life. A child who feels unloved may become hostile, and a hostile adult is difficult to live with and often a detriment to society.

We are all aware of a generation of people called "hippies" who had long hair and wore dirty clothes. They played guitars, slept on the streets, and did many things different from ordinary citizens. I wonder how many of these boys and girls experienced love in their homes. Love says, "I am willing to accept a person though I may reject his attitudes, habits, and life-style."

When I ask young people, "What is the one quality you want your dad to express above everything else?" they say, "I want my parents to understand me." We cannot understand fully an 8-year-old, a 12-year-old, or a 16-year-old, because there is much we have forgotten. But a child wants to know Dad is trying to understand him, and accepts him, even while disapproving of some of his actions.

Many kids run away from home because they feel rejected. Perhaps their parents couldn't stomach their life-style. Father-love appreciates a son's heartaches and problems, frustrations and fads, and all else that comes along. Many parents make tragic mistakes in not distinguishing between loving someone and loving what he does. Agape, the selfless love of the Scriptures, reaches out and accepts a person as he is, not for what he does nor how he looks.

One day at the beach my family was sharing a prayer time after breakfast, and my daughter gave me a great insight. We were talking about the qualities of a father and children's attitudes toward their fathers, and she said, "One thing I've learned is that at this age (14) I realize I must accept you as a person, not just as my parent." Imagine that: she saw me as more than her parent, a person with feelings and attitudes as special to me as hers are to her. She continued, "When I look back at some things I've done and said, I think, shame on me—did I do that?" Understanding me was helping her understand herself.

We need to look at both sides of our disagreements: the parents' side and the children's. Children are persons, not "just our kids." They have individuality we must respect and enhance.

When was the last time you told your child you love him or her? I know fathers who are too tough to say, "I love you." That father also has a hard time telling his wife he loves her. She's supposed to know that, because "I married you, didn't I?"

To be a healthy child and effective adult, love is essential. Some adults can't get along with other people because they grew up in homes where they were not loved and never learned how to love. When they have major problems and see a psychiatrist who traces their problems back to childhood, they say, "I never saw my mom and dad kiss each other. I never learned to express love."

Do you know how you are accepted by God,

Christian? The Bible says you are accepted in Christ, the Beloved. Not by your goodness, but by His love. The Holy Spirit sheds that same love in a believer's heart to share with others—including his children.

The fifth thing a father must do is *discipline*. He is instructed to "Withhold not correction from the child" (Prov. 23:13). Today a big problem in families is child abuse. Can you understand a man brutalizing a little child? This is a perversion of discipline, a practice passed on from generation to generation. Proper discipline is healthy as well as essential for children.

There are four mistakes to avoid in correcting children. First, do not expect perfection. As fathers, we may aim at perfection but we rarely attain it. When your standard demands that your child must make straight A's, you may fail your child emotionally even if he succeeds academically. Forced perfectionism breeds hatred, and that is far from inner perfection.

A good-looking high school senior, an average student but an outstanding athlete, broke down as he poured out his heart to me. "I can never please my dad. No matter what I do, he wants to know why I didn't do it better. I'm buried under his expectations. He wants me not only to be successful, but superior. I'm not interested in being superior; I just want to be me." I heard deep bitterness in his accusation: "He is certainly no example of success himself!" The father's heavy hand of discipline was crushing the boy's spirit and destroying his initiative. We must beware of the egotistical error of trying to achieve our personal ambitions through our children.

A second mistake is over-coercion. For example, when a child gets up in the morning and you say, "Wear that pair of shoes. Wear these socks. Brush your teeth. Did you wash your ears? Did you wipe your face? Come to breakfast. Sit down. Get up. Be sure you wipe your mouth before you go to school. Is your hair brushed well? Did you get your lunch? Be sure you are out there when the bus comes. Be home on time. When you get home, carry out the trash. The lawn must be . . . " And on and on.

We force our children into a state of anxiety and ineptness when we constantly goad with "Do this, do that." In self-defense, the child builds a habit of procrastination against the barrage.

Recently a fellow called me who was having a problem on his job because he refused to do what he was told to do. As we talked, I asked if procrastination was a problem with him, and he admitted it was. "I detest anyone telling me what to do," he said. In his growing years someone had made him hate commands, and he still couldn't handle them as an adult. No doubt the parents were not altogether to blame for their son's problem, but they unnecessarily saddled him with a heavy career handicap.

A third misuse of correction is excessive severity in punishment. Children have an innate sense of right and wrong, and they usually know when they deserve punishment. But undue harshness produces genuine moral outrage in children.

Continual violation of their sense of justice will foster callousness and a spirit of revenge. Many adults steamroll their way through society in unconscious retaliation against their parents.

A fourth aberration in discipline is withdrawal of love. When you say, "If that's the way you're going to be, don't expect any more help from me," you are cutting emotional ties even if the threat is never carried out. Nobody can stand strong after personal rejection by a parent.

"You're bad." "You won't amount to anything." "Why can't you be like your sister?" These personality attacks are devastating to one's self-image, and they betray utter lovelessness. Such victims find it extremely difficult to relate to people no matter how friendly they may be. I have seen 12-year-old children with thick walls around their soul because they have been hurt so much by their parents. Love is a powerful force both in its presence and its absence. Always discipline with love.

Sixth, *assign work* in training your children. Even when your child is 5 years old, give him a chore and reward him for completion. To do so is not teaching children to be materialistic but to be responsible. When he fails to do his task he loses his reward. Our free society was built on a system of fair compensation for competent effort, and our spiritual life has a similar promise of rewards for faithful service. As our welfare-bent society promotes the expectation of something for nothing, Christians must propagate the reality of our reaping as we sow. While some chores may earn money or some other prize, certain kinds of work should be done as contributions to the family. These are recognized and commended by the parents to teach service as well as the value of work. Children with no chores and no incentive to work will find the transition to a laboring world a formidable hurdle.

Seventh in your training campaign, *establish communication*. Communication means that you and your children hear each other—not only what is said but what is meant. This is important because people can't function together unless they communicate clearly, and our ability to communicate in today's society is dwindling steadily. Communication is more than an exchange of words.

There are times when our children need simply to express their feelings without the need of judgment or an opinion. A parent who senses this communicates concern even before saying anything. Being open to whatever your child feels gives a strong basis for mutual trust and helpfulness.

The communication gap sometimes results from a love gap. When two people love each other, they can talk through their difficulties. One child may be willing to talk to Mom about things that he would not talk to Dad about, and vice versa. That is one reason we have two parents.

Notice that Proverbs 22:6 says, "Train up a child (not children) in the way he (not they) should go." Children cannot be put in one category, because each one is different. Have you realized and appreciated this in your children? Each child is developing in a different way and at a different tempo. Each needs his father to respond to him in a different way. It is much simpler to gather them in a circle and say the same thing to all—but they all get varying messages because they hear from different perspectives.

Communication implies that I am willing to find out where each child is emotionally, spiritually, and physically and help him advance from there in God's plan. Communication also means that I persistently give and take until we feel right about each other and the channels are open for the next message.

The eighth step is to *encourage self-esteem.* Every person needs a good image of himself, not one of self-pride but of self-worth. Nothing builds up self-esteem in a child like the approval, compliments, and encouragement of a father. When he is not doing as well as you would like, look for the detail you can honestly praise and give suggestions, not criticism, for improvement. This is a love-in-action project.

Sometimes we forget that our children, even when college students and young adults, have feelings just as we do. To put them down because they have not reached our level of comprehension and skill is a thoughtless attack. We must realize their competence and make allowance for failure. Even when they deliberately do wrong, we can build rather than tear down by trying to understand the reasons, and by remembering the person is more important than his actions.

I constantly meet people whose self-image is 40 below zero, and I discover they never had the approval of their parents. Even when they did the best they could, it was never good enough. So they grew up thinking, "Why try?" If you don't value your child's initiative, creativity, and self-image, consistently put him down—then expect him to put you down when he gets big enough.

During a late evening chat, I shared with my teenage son my delight over his spiritual growth, and he said, "As far back as I can remember, you have been telling me something that has influenced my decisions." I could hardly wait to hear what it was, and he continued, "When I have a son, I'm going to tell him the same thing you keep telling me because it encouraged me and helped me to resist temptation. For years you have said, 'Andy, God loves you, and I believe He has something special for you.' " Evidently my son was hearing: "You are somebody; you are loved," and it made the difference.

The next lesson is *handling frustration*. For example, your child flunks a test and comes home from school with failure written all over his face. Do you say, "Not again!" or "That's tough, son, but we won't give up, will we?" Negative comments do not make a child positive. Through example and encouragement, children need to discover that problems need not be defeats.

A common adult hang-up is depreciating the problems of their children. Years of change have made us forget that a problem with a boyfriend or girlfriend can be a heartrending matter. Dad scoffs, "Puppy love—forget it." But suppose you and your wife went to a counselor with your problems and he said, "Don't fret, read the Bible, pray, and forget it." The treatment is similar in both cases. We tend to disregard our children as real people with real problems, frustrations, and anxieties.

Instead of offering a quick, simplistic solution, we need to help by showing that we care enough to listen and sympathize.

Try putting yourself in their place and ask yourself: "How would I have wanted my father to respond had I done that?" We fathers need to practice the golden rule at home: "Do unto your children as you would have your children do unto you." By understanding their problems and helping them through, we teach our children that frustrations can be stepping stones to achievement.

Further on in training *introduce the adult world* to your children. The world inhabited by grown-ups is infested with evil, strife, and dangers. Rather than shield children from all knowledge of these harmful influences, we must prepare them for dealing with this real, hard world.

In these days of economic strains there are financial problems in many homes. If there are problems, share them with your children. They will love you for being honest with them. They would like to see and feel that they could share some of your burden, to talk to the heavenly Father about some need that dad has. Expose them to the world that affects you and someday may touch them. And lead them in sensing our need of God and prayer.

Children face some choices that parents must not make for them. Teach them at an early age to ask God for guidance, and then stay with them through the struggle as they seek the will of God for their lives. Children who get ready-formed answers from their parents are adrift when they're suddenly on their own. Overprotection inhibits our children's maturing.

Naturally, a trainer-coach makes progress checks on his players. A corporation president uses all kinds of charts to track his operations. With a chart here and a graph there, he can tell you everything that is happening in his business. But he likely goes home and gives only passing thought to his child's progress. How careless and stupid can we get!

How do we keep a check on our children's progress? Not by reports and data, but by regular communication, concerned inquiries, and keen observation. You can't keep a scorecard, but you can keep in close touch.

The last training project I recommend may not sound like a task, but it is: *enjoy your children.* That seems easier than it is because we identify fun and games with enjoyment. That's a definite part of the scene where children are concerned, but there is much more.

When I asked my children, "What is it that you dislike about me the most?" they answered, "You're too serious." I realized I was too serious because I was preoccupied with something else, and I had to discipline myself to concentrate on having fun with my children!

But another aspect of enjoyment is appreciation, and I cannot appreciate my children unless I know them well and respect their individuality. That takes time and sometimes lots of patience. The training results show when your children show more and more appreciation of you and your values.

President Theodore Roosevelt was a dedicated family man as well as a conscientious statesman. He said, "The first essential for a man's being a good citizen is his possession of home virtues, based on recognition of the great underlying laws of religion and morality. No piled-up wealth, no splendor of material growth, no brilliance of artistic development, will permanently avail any people unless its home life is healthy."

6

Man, That's Love!

I believe the most misunderstood word in our vocabulary is *love*. The strife in our society and our homes illustrates our lack of understanding of this important word. From listening to the radio or watching television and reading books and magazines, it is painfully evident that men have counterfeited the true meaning of love. When a couple came to me for marriage counseling, the husband-to-be seemed so uneasy that I asked, "Do you really love this girl?" He answered unhesitatingly, "Why, sure I do." So I asked him to tell why he felt that he loved her. He replied, "She does something to me. I feel like a man in her presence. She's what I've been looking for. I think she's very attractive. I know my parents will be proud of me for having such a lovely girl as my wife . . . . " On and on he went, not mentioning a single thing that indicated his love *for her*, but only what she did *for him*. That is not love.

We have coined a phrase in this generation called "free love." We know what people mean by the term, but love is never free. All love costs somebody something. The idea of "free love" is the erroneous concept that you can give or receive the love you desire without involving yourself. The society is so jaded it does not know what real love is nor the accurate way to describe it.

A song we have sung for some time says, "What the world needs now is love, sweet love," but I'm not sure the modern version would help us much. Today's love songs speak a different language than the hymns of divine love and the old ballads that linked human devotion with sacrifice.

The message of the Bible communicates true love from Genesis to Revelation. This love encompasses both God and mankind, and it recognizes varied kinds of love.

In Ephesians 5 Paul talks about the quality, depth, and core of the total man's love for his family. Very bluntly he directs: "Husbands, love your wives even as Christ loved the Church and gave Himself for it" (v. 25). We husbands probably know what that means, and the staggering implications cause most of us to shrug our shoulders and look around for something more in the realm of possibility. But let's look more closely before we settle for less than God's best.

There are many humorous definitions of love. One of my favorites is:

Love is a very funny thing,
It's shaped just like a lizard,
It wraps its tail around your heart
And goes right through your gizzard.

That will get smiles but not many miles along the road of love. Others describe love like this: "A bell is no bell till you ring it, a song is no song till you sing it, and love is not love till it's given away." That poetry has a lot of truth, but it's still deficient as a definition of true love.

True Love

Let's try our own: Love is unselfish, tender, strong action reaching out to do what is best for another person. This is the purest concept of love, the agape love of God for His special creation, man.

Part of our confusion over the meaning of love arises from our use of one word for many kinds of love. We love a wife, mother, dog, chocolate candy, and success. If there were different words for all the kinds of love that we speak of, the dictionary would be considerably more complicated.

According to the Bible, love is a deep, meaningful emotion and action which God intends as a unifying factor in our lives. By love we are drawn together and united as one in spirit.

Have you explained true love to your children? They talk about it at school, read about it in books, and hear songs about it, but do they know your version—which I hope is God's version? Do you know how to tell them?

When you say, "Honey, I love you," do you mean "I like the way you look today" or possibly "You cooked a great breakfast"? Yes, love has different meanings.

Counterfeit Love

The sensitive man knows that there is a distinct difference between sex and love. Sex should include love, but often it does not. Many popular songs portray love as being little more than a kind of animal lust, beneath the dignity of personalities made in the image of God. Far from being love, illicit sex is a sin by which a man "destroyeth his own soul" (Prov. 6:32).

Not only single people are ignorant of true love. Married couples can express hostility or contempt in the sex act. Sex is made the expression of many things—but not according to God's plan. As it is the deepest intimacy between committed husband and wife, its perversion becomes the highest travesty against love.

A woman would like to live her whole life experiencing romantic love—and that's not shallow sentimentality because God made women to be loved. If you have lost all traces of your romantic days of courtship, you are a big loser. Sex, love, and romance are not always synonymous but they can be, and they are for the complete man.

Romantic love reaches out in little ways, showing attention and admiration. Romantic love remembers what pleases a woman, what excites her, and what surprises her. Its actions whisper: you are the most special person in my life.

Someone has said that in infancy a woman needs love and care, in childhood she needs fun, in her twenties she needs romance, in her thirties she needs admiration, in her forties she needs sympathy, and in her fifties she needs cash! The needs of a whole woman would more likely be the same in her fifties as in her infancy: love and care. This never changes.

One of the best descriptions of the romantic concept is expressed in this song:

Blow me a kiss across the room;
Say I look nice when I'm not.
Touch my hair as you pass my chair:
Little things mean a lot.
Give me your arm as we cross the street;
Call me at six on the dot.
A line a day when you're far away;
Little things mean a lot.

Give me your hand when I've lost the way;
Give me your shoulder to cry on.
Whether the day is bright or gray,
Give me your heart to rely on.
Give me the warmth of a secret smile,
To show me you haven't forgot;
For now and forever, for always and ever,
Little things mean a lot.

If you need help in discerning between true

* "Little Things Mean a Lot," Words/music by Edith Lindeman and Carl Stutz.
Copyright 1954, Leo Feist, Inc., New York, N.Y. Used by permission.

love and false love—perverted, distorted love—
ask this question: Will it help me become the
person God intended me to be? If the answer is
no, it is not true love.

The man who understands what God intends
him to be knows how he should treat his wife and
children. He understands that true love is love
from the heart. Love will express itself in many
ways to help a woman become the person God
intended her to be.

Some men give minks and diamonds to stir response from a woman; others try perfume and
pizza carryouts. The real response is inspired by
self-giving love from a man who is dependable
and responsible, someone who cares for her, protects her, and reaches out to her. His love gives
without looking for anything in return.

By the time we reach adulthood, many of us
have been playing games instead of loving for so
long that we don't realize that there is a better
way.

Love Games
One of the games is manipulating love. In this
disguised charade one marriage partner connives
to get his or her way while pretending that it's all
for the other's benefit. This kind of game hurts
both participants.

Then there is bartered love. "You give me that,
and I'll give you this," goes the bargaining.
Sometimes the game becomes a joke, but it has
sobering overtones. Barter in marriage suggests
something illegitimate or unworthy is traded, and

that kind of exchange often turns up duds. What began as a test of wits becomes a contest of spite.

A third game is conditional love. "Sure, I love you, but I loved you more when you got up mornings to fix my breakfast." Or, "How can I love a son who's afraid to fight for his rights?" Fickle love of this type is more a gamble than a game, and the dice are loaded against you.

Most of us knew some pain from conditional love as we grew up, but we learned to steer away from it.

I read recently about a man who discovered only in his late forties that he had loved his wife and children conditionally. Even his social contacts were conditioned on the basis that something be done for him. He revealed, "Because my love toward everyone else was based on a condition, I never felt forgiven by God or capable of ever deserving forgiveness. I grew up with parents who gave me everything on a conditional basis: I was to be good, obey them, and never embarrass them, to receive their favors."

Conditional love separates instead of uniting. People need to love each other for what they are, not for what they do, what they promise, or what they give. Unconditional love says, "I love you because *you are you.* No other condition is necessary."

A perverse kind of love game is dependency—obligation. It is subtly maneuvered by a parent claiming first place in a grown offspring's life. Despondency, loss of an inheritance, or threatened suicide may be ploys for holding a son or daughter from normal living. These parents are far too old for such silly games.

How does God love you? "God so loved the world that He gave His only begotten Son, that whosoever believeth in Him should not perish, but have everlasting life" (John 3:16). "Neither death, nor life, nor angels, nor principalities, nor powers, nor things present, nor things to come, nor height, nor depth, nor any other creature, shall be able to separate us from the love of God, which is in Christ Jesus our Lord" (Rom. 8:38-39).

That same love can flow from Christians to others because "the love of God is shed abroad in our hearts by the Holy Spirit which is given unto us" (Rom. 5:5).

Love Paupers

Some people find it very difficult to love. The person with a poor self-image has little love to share. Jesus said, "Love your neighbor as yourself," meaning, "Care for your neighbor as you care for yourself." But what does a person do who hates himself, in the sense of disliking what he is as a person? He's in trouble.

Do you have a hard time reaching out emotionally to someone else? Deep inside, you want to say, "I'd just like to tell you that I love you today," but you don't say it. We may fear to express our innermost beings because we have been hurt in the past by exposing our souls to others. We learned to be protective and cool to avoid hurt.

The most loving people in the world should be

God's people reaching out to each other, but we too are hung up on past rejection and regrets. Yet God sets us free to love by making us willing to suffer hurt and by giving us love that must be expressed. Are we open to this healing love?

Another type of person who has a hard time loving is one who is driven to excel in a job or a sport or another pastime. Our national spirit of competition and self-reliance propels ambitious boys and men upward with scant attention to secondary matters. Or an emotionally battered youth determines to prove his worth by his single-handed attainments.

Success for this love-starved man is measured by his accumulation of visible wealth and honors. He shows affection by bestowing costly gifts on others—and is bewildered when the recipients show only momentary appreciation. He doesn't realize his family wants his love above everything; someone must teach him how to love. Do you know anyone like this?

I believe that many married people today are confused about love to the desperate point of separation and divorce. They feel that they truly love each other but they have experienced only the game forms along with bittersweet tastes of erotic love. God has the solution.

The subject of love is deeper than an ocean. We all would do well to carefully and prayerfully examine our love relationships with family members. Are we displaying conditional love, bartered love, or manipulating love? Where can we start in loving openly, without fear of being hurt? We need to start where we are, and immerse ourselves deeper and deeper in God's kind of love—which covers a multitude of human frailties.

I hear people complain about competitors for their love. A wife, for example, often has to compete with sports. A frequent complaint is that the wife sits quietly on Sunday afternoon doing nothing while her husband and family watch a ball game. And Sunday is not the only day. Of course, this is only a symptom, not the real problem. But it is something the husband can specifically change to prove his wife counts more to him than entertainment.

Television in general may be your wife's competitor. Or perhaps it's a hobby that preoccupies many of your spare hours. Your wife would not say these are wrong in themselves, but she is diminished by them if she feels they have more of your attention than she does.

Third, even friends can be rivals to a wife. A man may express more kindness and give more time to good friends than to his wife. This is deeply painful, and no decent husband will knowingly inflict such wounds. Are any of these competitors in your household? Could your wife possibly feel—even if she wouldn't say it— "What's the use? I'm no competition for your friends, your hobbies, for television, for your job, for all the things you seem to love more than you love me"? If you sense that possibility, your next step is clear in developing real love in your home: give rainchecks to your wife's competitors and tell her face to face, "Darling, I'm sorry if some of my activities have crowded you out; you're more important to me than my_____, and from now on you're first." But be ready to catch her—she might faint! And be sure you mean to keep your promise—it won't be nearly as hard as you may fear.

Would you like to measure your real love, the godly variety? Read 1 Corinthians 13 in the *Living Bible,* and where it says, "Love is patient" read "*I* am patient," "*I* am kind," etc. Is there room for improvement? Don't be discouraged— the God of love is your sufficiency.

How did Jesus love the Church? He identified Himself with the Church, calling us His body. A man who loves his wife gladly identifies himself with her. The Lord Jesus Christ provides everything the Church needs; so should the husband provide for his wife, with God's help. The Lord Jesus Christ protects His people, and a loving husband protects his wife. Jesus Christ gave Himself to meet the spiritual needs of His bride, and a faithful husband gives of himself to meet his bride's deep emotional and spiritual needs.

If a man knows how to romance his wife, love her, build her up, and help make her the woman God wants her to be, no one benefits more than the husband himself. "Give, and it shall be given to you," Jesus promised. When a man loves his wife properly, she becomes more than he dreamed and far more than he deserves.

The greatest expression of Christ's love was His death on the cross for us. This was the epitome of selfless, generous, unlimited, match-less, measureless love. In so many words, Jesus says, "As I have loved you, so are you to love your wife." Impossible? We must remember Jesus' other words: "With men this is impossible; but with God all things are possible" (Matt. 19:26).

A man becomes this kind of lover by first fall-ing in love with Jesus Christ, the source of true love. Many Christians have been cleansed of their sin through faith in Christ, but they have not yet "fallen in love" with their Saviour and they are weak in love. Do you need to give your life wholly to Christ so you can be filled with His love? If so, you may pray: "Lord Jesus, I want to love my wife with my head, my heart, and my body to help her be the ultimate woman she can be; I offer my body first to you as a living sac-rifice, so I may prove the perfect will of God in my life. Amen."

7

The Openhearted Man

Have you heard about the loving husband who cleaned the house every Saturday morning while his wife slept in? For ten years he exerted his labor of love, never mentioned his selfless service. Imagine the husband's consternation when his wife finally exploded: "If you think I'm such a terrible housekeeper, why don't you clean the house every day!"

That story is probably fictitious, but it's not far from some real-life situations. It illustrates the importance of good communication between husband and wife. Industry spends millions of dollars annually to help employees communicate more effectively, but little is being done to alleviate the problem in the home. A group of psychologists I talked with traced incompatibility in many areas of home life to lack of communication.

To talk and listen with understanding is the simplest definition of communication. Listening is not passive; it is concentrated outreach with the ears and mind and heart to understand what another person is saying. We must go back to Genesis to get a clear picture of communication.

God's main purpose for creating mankind was for companionship. The first thing God improved on in the world He created was loneliness. He gave to Adam a wife to meet the need for constant human companionship. To fulfill this purpose in marriage, communication was an essential factor. For Adam and Eve to have real companionship, they had to communicate their deep, true feelings toward each other. In order for Eve to complete Adam and help him become the total man God intended, clear communication was indispensible. A breakdown in communication disrupts the flow of life.

Word Watching

The Bible says, "If any man offend not in word, the same is a perfect man." None of us is perfect, but it always helps to aim high. Throughout the Scriptures we are reminded of the power of words. Job complained to his friends, "How long will you vex my soul and break me in pieces with words?" (19:2) I wonder how many husbands and wives have felt like that. In Proverbs 18:21 we read: "Death and life are in the power of the tongue."

All through Scripture we see that what we say builds or destroys people. This is especially true for two people who live together intimately. Realizing that "the tongue can no man tame; it is an unruly evil, full of deadly poison" (James 3:8), we need to examine several things.

In personal relationships, it is important to communicate what we are feeling, our personal reactions. Someone has said that communication between husband and wife is an exploration of the depth of each other's feelings, an experience and adventure in each other's emotions.

Most communications are on a shallow level, never reaching the depths that God intended for honest sharing with others. While we cloak our feelings with glib words, underlying meanings sometimes slip out through our glances, our gestures, and our posture. Feelings can't be entirely suppressed.

Let's look at the conversation between Eve and Satan in the Garden of Eden. The devil said, "That's not what God said; or if He said it He didn't really mean it. You didn't understand God's words to you" (Gen. 3:5, paraphrased). Satan's twisting of communication had a critical part in man's loss of Paradise.

I saw a cartoon that read: "I know you believe you understand what you think I said, but I'm not sure you realize that what you heard is not what I meant." That sounds like both parties are confused. When you talk to someone, you may convey several of these six at once:

what you think you are saying

what you meant to say
what you actually said
what the other person heard
what the other person says about what you said
what you think the other person said about
    what you said.

When you say something to your wife, you think she heard it, but her mind was dealing with more than your actual words. Sometimes we say things casually and expect the listener to understand exactly what we meant. We take for granted that what we said, what we meant, and what we felt are understood. Miracles aren't that easy! The recipient of the message may understand one thing from our eyes, another from our gestures, and another from our mouth. When the transmission is not consistent in all forms, confusion or misunderstanding results.

When you consider some of your own communication problems with people you've known many years, you realize how difficult good communications are. No doubt you can recall more than one example in the current week!

As an experiment, give a set of simple instructions to your family, then ask them to whisper individually what you said. Much of the "playback" will be inaccurate.

Often the reason for our misunderstanding is that we filter speech through our own feelings and perspectives, leaving a different residue than the original. Sometimes we do not hear what is said because we are busy preparing our rebuttal to the incoming message. Two people who are living with each other the rest of their lives have a high stake in communication.

Sometimes our problem is inability to put our feelings in words. A person says, "I know how I feel, but I don't know how to express it." Aside from a refresher course in the English language (which would benefit many Americans), I recommend daily practice and lots of patience. Acquiring verbal skill takes work.

Isn't it true that most marriages play the cat-and-mouse game? We run from each other verbally and emotionally when we ought to be willing to express what we feel as honestly as we know how. Failure to communicate widens the emotional distance between us.

After years of counseling, I am convinced that a prominent cause of broken marriages is the suppression of true feelings. Estranged couples have never learned to express and accept the innermost feelings of their hearts. For fear of hurting the partner or exposing a personal weakness, feelings are submerged until a crisis forces an explosion that shatters more than illusions. The sudden shock unnerves everyone, but the cause has existed all along.

Married couples should learn to communicate about everything early in marriage. I remember the first problem of communication I had with my wife. It was during our honeymoon at a cottage on Lake Lure in North Carolina. She cooked our first meal, and we sat down to a delightful fried chicken dinner. I looked around and asked, "Where is the gravy?" She said, "We never had gravy with chicken." I said, "I never had chicken *without* gravy." She rose quietly from the table and made at least a gallon—not knowing exactly how to make gravy, she kept adding too much of various ingredients! It was more like jello than gravy, but she learned in time. I could have sulked and wondered: "When is she going to learn how to fix a real meal?" but I spoke up and she responded. I've enjoyed a lot of fried chicken with gravy since then!

Inner Circle

Let's look at five levels on which we communicate—I like to think of them as circles rather than levels. The outermost circle of communication where we are the safest is the circle of clichés: "How are you doing? Glad to see you. Looking fine. Hope you're feeling well. How's your family?" That says nothing. You neither learn anything nor feel anything.

The second circle of communication is repetition of facts. "Did you hear about this?" or, "The news today is pretty grim." It conveys publicly known information about events.

The third circle evidences willingness to express your own judgments or ideas: "His statement was very critical." "I won't vote for that."

Deeper yet is the frank expression of your feelings: "To be honest, honey, I feel a little hurt."

The innermost circle of communication bares the heart with no ulterior motives; it seeks peace with a conscience at peace.

Many marriages never pass the third circle of

communication: they are willing to talk about places, things, and ideas, but shrink back from personal involvement. Little contact of spirit with spirit is made.

Men may be insensitive to needs of their families because they don't really hear them. In many cases our families do not know how to communicate with us. And when they do we are not listening. We hear basic facts. For example, if your wife says, "I don't feel well," she may mean, "Honey, take me in your arms and hold me tight." If we only receive facts and don't reach the innermost feelings, we often miss the real message. A strong marriage is built on the knowledge of feelings that are indeed facts.

You've heard about those rare times when the Bell Telephone System's wires get crossed and numerous customers are speaking nonsense to perfectly intelligent people. Frustration, anger, and helplessness erupt, and a good deal of important business goes undone. The effects are similar in some husband-wife communications, with the added complication of not recognizing the problem or sensing how to solve it.

Most men retreat instinctively from emotion. We quickly lose our moorings in a storm of tears, and we do not understand that emotional storms rise from deep springs though they pass swiftly. Emotions embrace important meanings, often inexpressible ones, and if we unemotional males are to live wisely and productively with our mates we must meet them at the deepest expression of their needs. Tears usually are a cry for tenderness, not talk, but they are a sign that discussion and understanding are needed to resolve a problem. It is an opportunity for the husband also to open his heart—softly.

Recently I was repeating the marriage vows to a couple, and in the middle of the ceremony I realized that nowhere are there any "if's." "I take thee to be my wedded wife, to have and to hold from this day forward, for better, for worse, for richer, for poorer, in sickness and in health, till death do us part." Marriage is a contract—but also a relationship. It is an emotional as well as volitional giving of one to the other. Have you fulfilled your emotional commitment to your wife?

Helps and Hindrances

Look out for these helps and hindrances concerning communication. First, the hindrances.

Busyness threatens good communication. When the pace of life gets hectic, the finer things often get trampled. Slow down in the home stretch, husband!

Impatience garbles communication. Emotional irritation puts fuzziness in the transmitter and static in the receiver. Take three deep breaths before speaking in a tense situation, and you'll save a lot of breath.

If communication takes our best effort, preoccupation with other goals turns us away from the target. Most of us can do only one thing at a time well—be sure to give time to communicating with your wife.

Insensitivity is a shell that deflects communication, while sensitivity is a mirror that catches even shadows. The Holy Spirit indwelling you is the Supreme Communicator. He communicates the murmur of your spirit to the heavenly Father, and likewise can communicate what you feel to your wife; pray that the Father of spirits will sensitize your spirit.

"Safe" subjects may be a hindrance to you. Do you subconsciously avoid conversational areas that have produced fireworks in the past? These subjects must be cleared up if you are to know and care for each other at the deepest level.

Children are often a hindrance to communication. When I hear parents say, "We've never left our children," I want to tell them what they have missed. Even when children are young, they should be put to bed early so that you and your wife can talk alone and learn about each other. You might be surprised to find a different person in a quiet hour and place, especially if your children are still preschool age. Every couple should get away regularly from their children to nurture their own fellowship.

A strong streak of independence is a hindrance for some couples. A young lady who talked to me about getting married admitted a pride in independence which she realized was a problem. Independence implies, "I only need you for the ordinary things; don't try to possess all of me." This reservation seriously impairs the sharing of life that God intended for marriage. Two remain two instead of becoming one.

Hypocrisy is another hindrance—we call it sophistication or dignity, not letting our real feelings show. It is possible you have avoided this modern masking of self, but most of us find ourselves at times pretending to be better than we are. This easily extends into family life, covering our real selves. Though our intention is good, the effect is alienating. To be free we need to be completely honest.

If you have not communicated deeply, you may fear being rejected by your mate. You fret: "What will he think if I tell him what I really feel?" The Bible says that perfect love casts out fear. A loving relationship cannot develop steadily when a couple is afraid to express what they feel. If you and your wife trust each other, you can talk about your goals, what pleases you most, and what hurts you most. You may proceed slowly in exploring new depths, but keep moving forward and the joy and excitement in your relationship will be released.

Fortunately, there are also helps for good communication. They are positive steps which ward off the hindrances.

Speak clearly. This is partly a mechanical matter of enunciation and partly a matter of taking time to see that your message is heard. Respect and consideration are shown by careful speech, and the attention of the listener escalates.

Speak until your message gets through—gently. We men want to retreat or sulk when the conversational weather gets turbulent. But the sun shines on the far side of the squall, and husband and wife need to go through it together. Patience pays handsomely.

Strive to understand your wife more than you seek to be understood by her. This outgoing effort will generate big dividends as your wife responds from her heart.

Another action that helps is to plan times together—time for talking and observing each other's interests. Sharing activities opens new insights and deeper appreciation.

Comparatively few couples discover the growing closeness of praying together. I believe the highest level of communication often comes when two people talk to God together. As you learn to communicate sincerely with God, you experience a growing identification with your spouse's concerns. Sometimes we will say things about ourselves in prayer that we would not say with our eyes open. During prayer your marriage partner picks up the love in your heart, the humility, the spiritual aspirations, and divine love draws the praying couple closer.

Develop one or more mutual interests. This may require a sacrifice of preferred pastimes, but the resulting companionship will strengthen the sense of oneness and the awareness of how to meet each other's needs. Start small if necessary, but find something you both like and make it a team project.

Emotional Maturity

God gave the husband and wife to each other to make them more than they could be singly. The completion of each cannot take place until they learn to share their innermost being and work for the good of the other. The personal areas that are kept private have no opportunity for growth. Why not try God's plan?

Marriage, love, and communication cannot be separated from God without shriveling them. There may be numerous areas of your life that you mark "off limits" to God as well as to your wife. Could they include fear of inadequacy, deeply rooted bitterness, feigned love, or a spirit of revenge? These are poisons in the soul that God and your mate can help dispel—if you seek help.

God seeks to develop your soul as well as your body. Many personable people are not using all their God-given gifts because their emotional life is constricted. They refuse to allow their emotions to be exposed and to be brought to maturity. Examine yourself for a moment; are you courageous enough to look inward to see what is really there? Then are you willing to talk to God and your wife about your hidden self? Little by little, you may be strengthened until you will care to say: "Honey, tell me exactly what you feel about me, about yourself, everything" and not say a word until she finishes! Only a real man can do that.

We men want to be masculine. A man has—or should have—emotions in the soul as well as muscles in the body. If you have not matured in this part of your being, pride or fear may be your enemy. Open your heart to the light of God and the sympathy of your mate, and you will see the enemy retreating. The fullness of emotional development and interrelationships can be yours.

I challenge you to take these steps to deep communication, first privately and then together. You can know the person you married at the depth of her being as you learn together. Your marriage, your family, and your relationship to God and to others will move toward their fullest potential as you speak and live from the heart.

8

Jesus' Man

The last clause of 1 Corinthians 2:16 expresses an incredible thought: "We have the mind of Christ." In this passage the Apostle Paul explains the attitude of his own heart and moves on to speak of the source of his wisdom and knowledge. In essence he said, "Unlike the wise men of this world, our wisdom came not from our experiences or our study but from the Spirit of God who 'indwells us, giving us the mind of God."

Is that possible? Our non-Christian friends consider us very human, and we ourselves are very aware of our limitations. What does Paul mean when he says Christians "have the mind of Christ"?

I have challenged you to courageously open your heart to your wife, and if you are not able to do that, the reason is that you have not fully opened your heart or spirit to God. Your basic problem is spiritual. Every Christian has "the mind" of Christ because Christ lives within him, but many Christians have not fully opened their mind to Christ for His renewing work.

The total man is not a perfect man; he is a maturing man, a striving man, a studying man, a knowledgeable man. He has not arrived at his goal, but is on his way to becoming the husband his wife needs and the father his children need. He is a man on the most exciting journey of his life. He is learning to be a balanced man and the total man God created him to be.

No doubt you have thought, "I just can't be all these things. I can't live up to the level of loving that you are talking about. I am not capable of the communication you are talking about, of understanding my family, of giving them my time." You may have told your wife that you are ashamed of the way you have lived. You may have confessed to your children that you have not been the father you should be but would like to be. Your repentance and desire are important to God for His further working in you.

If you have been aiming toward God's ideal, your family undoubtedly has prayed for spiritual growth in your life. Your wife, no doubt, has spotted evidences of your attempt to be thoughtful of her needs. More than likely, your sons and daughters have said, "I believe something is happening to Dad." You have received encouragement from their words.

Everything we've considered so far in becoming a total man hinges on this basic principle: the complete man is a spiritual man. Here I want to give you some characteristics of the spiritual man.

In 1 Corinthians 2:14 Paul says that "the natural man receiveth not the things of the Spirit of God: for they are foolishness unto him: neither can he know them, because they are spiritually discerned." Many of the principles we have discussed are found in good psychology, but the deeper principles of relationship with God and with people are found in Christian theology, the study of God and His creation.

The Apostle Paul says the "natural man" cannot begin to understand God's basic truths. Paul means that the man who has been born physically but not spiritually is cut off from communicating with God and he cannot perceive the knowledge and wisdom of God—they are foolish to him.

The Right Start

The first step to real manhood is spiritual rebirth—"You must be born again" (John 3:7). By nature, you are spiritually dead, for "your iniquities have separated between you and your God" (Isa. 59:2). You must believe that Jesus went to the cross to die for your sins. When you tell Jesus that His death on the cross was sufficient payment for your sins and ask Him to come into your heart to forgive you, cleanse you, and indwell you, Jesus Christ comes into your life at that moment. The most crucial need of every family is a father whose heart is indwelt by Christ.

The husband is the head of his home, but until Christ comes into his heart he cannot be their spiritual guide. And if the father is not the spiritual head, the home has no spiritual leader and is threatened by many dangers. When the man of the house is reborn and spiritually alive to God, he has the indwelling Christ to help him become the total man he needs to be.

Friend, if you are without Christ, you have deprived your family of the one thing they need above everything else—spiritual leadership. Your wife could wrap all of your wealth in a bundle and sink it in the ocean and still be rich and secure if she has a man whose life is balanced because it is directed by God, a man who can take care of her physically, emotionally, and spiritually. There is no substitute for a saved husband and father.

Leader of the Leader
The second need for a spiritual man is to allow God to lead him. Every family needs a father and every wife needs a husband who gets his daily directions from God. When your family understands that you are living in the will of God, you will not find your decisions challenged so vigorously. Your allowing God to lead you builds their confidence in you as their spiritual leader. Observing your dependence on God will help them to also depend on Him. There is no finer wisdom you can pass on to your children.

Young children following a spiritual father should be talking to the Lord about what they should do with their lives and about their future marriage partners. They should be forming the habit of asking the Lord to help them. Decisions based on sound human reasoning are not adequate for spiritual success; God must be a part of truly successful living.

Bring God and your family together in decision-making as a normal procedure. I tell my family, "We must wait on the Lord," or "Let us wait on that and pray together." Later I may ask, "Do you feel like God has said anything to you?" And I don't laugh if one of the younger ones says, "I haven't heard God say anything." I just say, "That's all right. You may not understand for awhile, but God is in the process of teaching you. If you follow me as I follow the Lord, God can transfer that lesson through me to your heart."

Some of the most precious moments in our home are those in which we are all kneeling in prayer together seeking God's mind. It is exciting to see who will first receive the clear guidance we need.

Dad, you can give your children everything else in the world, but if you don't give them a father who has accepted Jesus Christ as Saviour and is allowing Him to lead in decisions, attitudes, and actions, you will never become all the man God wants you to be.

The Pause That Rebuilds
The third thing necessary for becoming a

spiritual man is to have regular private devotions. We can tell our children repeatedly to read the Bible and pray, but the simplest and most effective way to teach them this spiritual principle is to do it ourselves. A father cannot leave this teaching to his wife. You may say, "I travel and I'm seldom at home." Even if you are not at home very often, your family needs to see you do it when you are. When a child sees his father reading the Bible and praying on his knees, the memory will be irrevocably stamped on his impressionable mind.

I want to ask you, Dad: When was the last time your children saw you on your knees with an open Bible, seeking direction from God?" That's an unmistakable lesson to a child. To be a spiritual man you must take time to talk to Him and to listen to Him through His Word. The regularity of this meeting, not its length, is the important thing. When you're running late, I suggest you pause long enough to get on your knees and tell the Lord, "I am committing this day to you. Late as I am, I am not leaving this house without getting on my knees before You." God will reward that commitment.

The homes of fathers who are doing this are richly blessed. God is bringing them toward maturity because they are taking spiritual steps each day. If you can pause for only a prayer of commitment and a memorized Bible verse, that will launch you into the day and a later opportunity for a longer period of meditation and reading.

Your attitude of mind covers your home. When

your attention is focused on Bible truths, you are exercising the mind of Christ, His thinking. When I think as Christ thinks, I am loving my wife and children more faithfully; I am more sensitive to the needs of those around me. Apart from the principles of the Bible, you cannot be the man, the husband, and the father you may be.

Insight in Action

The fourth essential to becoming a spiritual man is an awareness of the spiritual needs of your family. A spiritual man is able to discern beyond the visible. When he listens to his children, he hears what they say and he feels what they feel. The Bible says that Jesus confronted people and knew them inside and out. We do not have Christ's mind to that degree, but we increasingly have His sensitivity, and as we live together in love our minds are open to each other's needs.

A father who is filled with the Spirit of God can readily discern the basic spiritual needs of his family. When members of the family become frustrated or angry, they need spiritual counsel from their spiritual head, the father. When fathers come home after work, they need to have their antennas out to read what their wife and children are thinking. Mom's saying everything is "fine" does not lessen the husband's responsibility to discern and measure the spiritual growth of the family day by day.

Dad, if you are not a member of a vibrant church, a fellowship where the Spirit of God is moving and where your family can grow spiritually, you need to change your membership. You are responsible for the spiritual progress of your family. When you see your children drifting, you are responsible for anchoring them to the solid rock of faith. Families need a church where they are taught the Scriptures, have fellowship with the people of God, and learn to share their faith. The right church is your great helper in building the right kind of home.

A family visited our church several Sundays who were at the time members of a very liberal and rather spiritually dead fellowship. With a congregation of over 7,000 I was not looking for more members, but was genuinely concerned about this family. I encouraged the father to take his family to a Bible-centered church, wherever he might choose. He waited two years to make a decision, and then only after both of his teen-agers had almost wrecked their lives. He and his wife came forward during the invitation one Sunday morning and tearfully shared with me, "Pastor, we finally made the decision, but I'm afraid we waited too long."

That kind of procrastination occurs far too often. Are we more concerned about the reactions of fellow church members than the needs of our children? They need the umbrella of a Bible-teaching pastor and fellowship.

The Serving Leader
The fifth thing you should notice about the spiritual man is that he is alert to opportunities for service. He is alert to the opportunity of serv-

ing his family. I regret that I was a long time learning this. I thought my family was supposed to serve me, the father, the husband, the pastor. When it dawned on me that it was my responsibility to serve my family, my whole life changed.

A spiritually minded man will always be alert to opportunities for serving his family. Would you like your son to grow up to be the kind of husband who cares for his wife? How is he going to learn? By reading books? No, by watching his dad. A spiritually-minded man has the discernment of the Holy Spirit; he senses opportunities for serving his wife and children.

God has shown me what He meant about serving the family. It is my responsibility to submit myself to their needs and to see that those needs are being met. It may simply be that a daughter needs help with algebra. You say, "My son can help her." That is not all she needs. She needs a tender, caring father. Dad, you may not know the first thing about algebra, but it is not how much you know, rather your willingness to offer your help that causes your child to appreciate you.

You may ask, "How does this fit in with a wife being submissive to her husband?" If you want to motivate her to be submissive, serve her (*not subject her to yourself*) by meeting her needs; assume leadership, and let God work out her submission.

The Available Leader

The sixth characteristic of this spiritual man is that he will be available to share himself with others. Because he is unselfish, he has a desire to give of himself without expecting anything in return. The joy of giving motivates him to pour himself into his family.

From the time that my children were small, I have made an effort to have a brief chat and prayer with them before they go to sleep each night. Now they are teenagers, and we are still having nightly chats, though often much longer and more involved. Because of my schedule, I sometimes miss a session, but not if I can help it. There is something very special about being there to listen and pray shortly before they go to sleep. Because they are relaxed and confidential, they often will share things not accessible at another time. My being there says, "I care. I am interested in you. I love you."

A pastor friend of mine is one of a family of seven children. His father, a pastor too, was very busy and away from home until late night after night. But no matter how late he came home, he always knelt by the bed of each child to pray. My friend said he could recall lying quietly as though he were asleep many nights and hearing his father whisper a prayer for him. He said his father's presence for those brief moments always served to calm his spirit. Often when he was tempted during the day, a mental picture of his father kneeling by his bed acted as a bulwark against Satan's invasion into his life. Is it any wonder that all of those children are happily married, and that four of the five sons are pastors?

Sharing ourselves with our family is time wisely

invested, sure to bring rich rewards. "For what-soever a man soweth, that shall he also reap" (Gal. 6:7). But remember that we reap whatever we sow, more than we sow, and later than we sow. The principle of sowing and reaping applies to families just as much as to farming.

Not only should a father share himself with his family, but he should learn to share his faith with others. A father sharing with his family how the Lord used him to lead someone to Christ does more to motivate his wife and children to share their Christian testimony than all the study courses combined. The memory of a godly father will spiritually motivate children to duplicate their father's actions and attitudes.

By demonstration and by instruction we should teach our children as early as possible to give money to God through the church, not just to meet a church budget but as an act of love for God in obedience to His Word. Money is an essential factor in everyone's life; therefore the way to handle money is an important lesson for children. Father, that responsibility and opportunity belongs to you.

Learning to give to God can become an exciting family affair. Recognizing a need together, and giving and praying toward God's supplying that need are practical and joyful experiences. These lessons, well taught, will provide a lifetime of financial and spiritual guidance for your children.

Many families cannot avoid some financial difficulty, but the strength to persevere and to work through them comes from honoring God in our use of money. A tithing father is investing in the financial and spiritual welfare of his family.

The Spiritual Guardian

The last thing I want to note about a spiritual man is that he abhors everything that threatens the welfare of his family. He will be cautious about the type of television programs his children watch. He will not approve literature of bad taste nor jokes that imply unkindness or impurity. He is aware that what enters the mind remains there, to elevate or to degrade. He realizes that if he doesn't protect his family from the destructive forces of society, no one will.

At times a spiritual man may seem too strict, but he will try to keep a good balance. Lovingly he will correct attitudes and habits that develop which may disrupt the harmony of the home. He will not act as a policeman, spying on every activity and telephone call, but as a caring father who desires the best for his family.

No doubt you question how any man can live up to all these responsibilities. By himself he cannot, and since no one is perfect, the goal always remains ahead of us. But the possibilities are far greater than most of us imagine—when we take the right steps.

Do you truly desire to be the husband your wife needs? Do you really want to be the father your children need? I believe you do if you have read this far. And where do you begin?

Right where you are. If you have never received Jesus Christ into your heart through repentance and faith, you begin there. The Scripture says, "If thou shalt confess with thy mouth the Lord Jesus, and shalt believe in thine heart that God hath raised Him from the dead, thou shalt be saved. For with the heart man believeth unto righteousness; and with the mouth confession is made unto salvation" (Rom. 10:9-10). The first step to becoming the total man—the loving husband, the caring father—that your family needs is to ask Jesus Christ into your life as Saviour and Lord. The moment you do that, the Bible says the Holy Spirit will come into your life to abide there forever as your Guide, Teacher, Comforter, and Power. Read John 14 through 16 for Jesus' illumination on this.

God has promised to be your constant helper as a husband and a father—have you trusted Him for that? Are you daily reading your Bible, praying, and obeying God's Word? You will not build spiritual muscles without feeding your soul and exercising your spirit. Begin there if that's where you are. Ask God for a spiritual partner—your wife or a Christian friend—if you need encouragement to walk in God's path. Seek, ask, knock persistently, and God will open the doors to spiritual prosperity and power.

I challenge you, husband: take one spiritual step toward God today, and He will clearly mark your next step to true manhood and godly leadership in your family.